HELMAR

The Master Key BrainCharger

HELMAR RUDOLPH

The Master Key BrainCharger

A PREMIUM MASTER KEY SYSTEM STUDENT WORKBOOK

Published by JAH Holding, Inc.

»The Master Key BrainCharger«
A Premium Master Key System Student Workbook

By Helmar Rudolph

Published by JAH Holding, Inc.
Cover Design: Markus Dahlenburg, Miesbach, Germany

Website: www.MasterKeySystem.tv
Deutsch: www.MrMasterKey.com
Twitter: www.twitter.com/mrmasterkey
Facebook: www.facebook.com/mrmasterkey
Youtube: www.youtube.com/mrmasterkey

© JAH Holding, Inc. - All rights reserved.
Second Edition, April 2014

ISBN-10: 145639696X
ISBN-13: 978-1456396961

Printed in the USA by CreateSpace.com

INTRODUCTION

Welcome, Namaste, In La'kech!

The Master Key System is a self-study service. It requires a large degree of discipline and determination. To many a student, things – especially in the beginning – are not obvious. The Master Key BrainCharger makes them obvious.

This is it: The Master Key System provides you with ancient wisdom wrapped into very precise language. The BrainCharger explains, tests, motivates and encourages. The only missing element is: you. Welcome!

In order for you to deepen your understanding about the Master Key System, I have developed this workbook. It will document your progress and test your knowledge. I have also summarised each part for you, and explained each of the exercises where I deemed fit. I have provided personal book recommendations and – for the first parts – added some simple and fun exercises, too. I would like you to note that all these sprang from my mind, and as a result are based on my consciousness with its own breadth and limitations.

You are most welcome to answer only what you feel like answering – there is no obligation. It's not about satisfying me, only yourself. After now seven years of Master Key System practice, I'm here to share my insights with you, helping you achieve more – and hopefully faster.

People often want reassurances before they embark on something new. Well, the Master Key System doesn't promise anything, nor does it function in the traditional sense. It explains Universal Laws and Cosmic Principles, and how you can bring yourself into alignment with them. If you do, it's **you** that functions – or rather creates – well, and create you shall indeed.

It's your understanding and application of these laws and principles that will turn your life around, not just on an intellectual level, but tangibly. This won't happen overnight. It's a gradual process that never really ends, but neither does your life. One new insight and exercise at a time, you will gain the necessary strength to make your dreams come true. After all, that's why we are here, living and experiencing this life, preferably in its more evolved forms.

From our current perspective, the Universe is expanding, and so are the Solar System and Planet Earth. We, too, are expanding, reaching higher planes and realms with each life we live. Even in this one we can effect changes beyond our wildest dreams. It requires discipline, diligence, silence, repose, trust in the process, and self-confidence, but most of all honesty and an openness towards yourself in a world where change is the only constant. At the bottom of each dream or ideal, however, lies a scientific method which - if adhered to and obeyed - will make those dreams come true. I wish you all the best on this amazing journey into the depths of your own divinity – your infinite potential.

Remember that you have to be able to receive in order to actually receive. New concepts and ideas are, well, *new*. While your brain initially struggles to accept them for lack of existing patterns, time and exercise will create new neuropathways, and new synapses will fire. You will - quite literally - be born again. What once sounded strange and foreign, if not impossible, has now found a welcome entrance into our consciousness, and is about to turn into reality. Make the most of this amazing structure set up by the Great Architect of the Universe.

The Master Key System is an incredibly powerful tool and should be handled with respect and reverence. Enjoy the coming weeks and months, and may this workbook help you make the most of your studies. Should you require additional assistance, please use my website as a starting point.

Enjoy and prosper!

HELMAR RUDOLPH
CAPE TOWN, SOUTH AFRICA, APRIL 2014

Please affix here a photo of yourself

9x13 cm (3.5x5.11") format

I, _____, herewith declare, that today, the ____ day of _____, in the year _____, marks the beginning of my Master Key System Study Service. I will conduct my study in a professional manner and will be finishing it in a timely manner.

So be it!

1

One Consciousness, One Power

"One Consciousness, One Power" is the title of this first part. You are at the beginning of an amazing and richly rewarding journey. All you have to do is lay the claim, ask the question, desire it, pray – call it whatever you like.

You are going to explore the depths of your own Being. You are about to discover much light, but also some shadow, for one cannot exist without the other. The shadow, however, is just that: a shadow. In itself it's nothing without the light. As you are learning to let your light shine brightly, you reach higher, more joyful and abundant planes of existence. Welcome!

This course will assist you in empowering yourself. At the same time you will do this to others, and by creating a new kind of Man we are advancing, even redefining evolution.

If you want to get more wealth, health or happiness, you have to give it first. Giving is largely a mental process. By giving to others, you develop a consciousness for giving, because **what you pay attention to, you become conscious of** – and what you become conscious of takes up more and more space in your life. As you reach higher levels of understanding and appreciation for everything abundant, powerful, beautiful, healthy and loving, all this starts returning to you, because creation is subject to law. It's also called *resonance*.

You will learn in this part that there is only one Consciousness. When this Consciousness thinks, it shows in the myriad of visible and invisible forms. The purpose of spirit is to create matter, and through this process it experiences itself, only to return to its origin, which is once again spirit.

You will learn in this part that you are part of this one Consciousness, and that thinking is the connection between you (the part) and the whole.

The Master Key System will strengthen your rational and logical thinking, and will make it methodical and systematic. We all have thoughts all the time anyway, but here we are talking about real, truthful thinking – thinking with a specific aim in mind; prolonged and persistent thinking in the Silence; thinking that is systematically, constructively and harmoniously directed by yourself. But before we get there, we have to master the basics, and this is what this part is all about.

You will require a large degree of discipline for this study. Do yourself the favour and finish this course, no matter what, because an almost magical transformation takes place as you delve deeper into this subject.

You will become more aware of the small things, the finer details, the things you previously didn't pay any attention to. You will reduce or eliminate your (subconscious) judgment and see things as they are and for what they are. The next step is that you will be more careful with regards to your verbal expression. This is followed by an increased control of your emotions. And finally, you will think twice before you start doing things. These small steps combined imbue you with a power and force to be reckoned with. Remember that you will first have to give before you can receive it, so your aim should always be to be in service of others, to enrich their lives consciously and systematically. How? By the power of your thought and your clear intentions. Have the intention and then feel as if it has already happened! That's the secret, but more on that later.

With this study you will become more peaceful, balanced, and sovereign. Now imagine this happening to your entire family as you study together, or to your friends and colleagues. Step by step, the atmosphere becomes calmer, friendlier and more supportive. By giving to each other, you amplify this energy, and thus "much" leads to "more".

Now onto the practical part: read each part slowly and carefully. This should take you about 40-50 Minutes. Then do the exercise. Let me repeat: DO THE EXERCISE! It's through the exercise that you will be equipped with new abilities and skills, not by just reading the text. The reading deepens your understanding, but the exercise changes your "Being", because with it you are "doing" something, and practice makes perfect! Continuous action creates habits. Habits become automatic. Once automatic, you - in the truest sense of the word - don't have to *think about it* anymore. It has become part of your Subconscious Mind, and it is being executed without further conscious input on your behalf. Please reread these last two sentences, because they are *a key* to materialization and accomplishment – to health, wealth and happiness!

ABOUT THE EXERCISE

The exercise takes about 20-30 minutes. Try to practice it every day. Choose one particular room and place that you will be using for the next six months. This is important, as you are telling your body that "now is my time for studying the MKS". This builds routine, prepares yourself and makes your study more efficient. If you cannot be in one particular place all the time, relax; what you do is more important than where you do it.

The object of the exercise is to obtain **physical control**. This first exercise is the basis for all the others, because for the next six months you will be doing a lot of sitting still. The MKS exercises are about mental and physical control and relaxation (1-4), visualisation (5-11), as well as concentration and contemplation (12+). You may already notice the system underlying the exercises. They help you become more capable of creating mental images, of visualising your ideal life. Remember that concentration means a focussed and continuous attention, or awareness. Remember that this expands your consciousness. This forms habits, which become automatic, and then become "you". The circles closes once again.

Students often ask: "*When do I know that I have obtained physical control?*" Well, in this exercise it's more about sitting still for some time rather than being able to control every cell of your body. So take it easy and perhaps start with a few minutes, but increase it every day by 3-4 minutes, and by the end of the week, you can sit still without moving for half an hour. Nothing happens overnight; it takes time and practice.

I'd like to close with a quote from Part One: "*We cannot express powers that we do not possess. The only way by which we may secure possession of power is to become conscious of power, and we can never become conscious of power until we learn that all power is from within. When you know the Truth and express only the Truth, only truthful and thus beneficial things will happen to you.*"

This, and always remember this, is the Master Key in brief. You will learn to become a conscious channel that expresses in form that which already exists as potential in the Universal. Which form it takes is subject to law, and dependent on how you think about life. The stronger you become, the more capable you will be in breaking old habits and patterns - those that didn't serve you in the past, and brought you to where you are today. These habits or patterns now serve you in transforming them, transmuting or transcending them. So it is you who is doing the transformation, and you are doing it in an ever more powerful way. Then, over time, you will be able to express powers you didn't even think existed.

CHECKLIST

1. Please write down in keyword form the changes that you have recognized taking place in your mind. (Example: you caught yourself having a negative thought and asked yourself why you were thinking it and whether you really had to think it.)

2. Write down the 3 most important things you have learnt from this part.

    1.
    2.
    3.

3. Write down how you intend applying this newly gained knowledge in your daily life.

4. Check those items that apply or that you have performed this week.

    ☐ Another person has changed its behaviour towards me in a

positive way.
- [ ] I have changed my behaviour towards another person or situation.
- [ ] I remained calm in an undesirable situation.
- [ ] I have consciously taken note of something that I wasn't aware of in the past.
- [ ] Before taking a decision, I stopped and asked myself what the outcome would be like.
- [ ] I have looked at something common with completely eyes and noticed the change in my own interpretation.
- [ ] A new person has entered my life, and we are getting on well.
- [ ] Someone unexpectedly gave me a present.
- [ ] I have stroked an animal or a plant and have spoken to it.
- [ ] I have become aware of my own breath flow.
- [ ] I have done something that somebody else really enjoyed.
- [ ] Before going to sleep, I gave thanks to all the beautiful things that happened day, or those I learned from.

5. Write down one thing that you wish for in life at this present moment. Make it short. Then write down how you would feel if this dream became true. Then spend some time observing and delving into the feeling itself.

6. Indicate how much closer you have come to this dream by applying what you've learnt this week.

    - [ ] Dream fulfilled.
    - [ ] Got a lot closer.
    - [ ] Somewhat closer.
    - [ ] Need to work a bit more on my thinking.

7. Write down the obstacles that you think are in the way of fulfilment and how you intend removing them. (Review your answer same time next week.)

8. Write down those things that you were grateful for this week. (**Hint:** *Make it a habit of reviewing the day before you go to sleep and call to mind everything you can be grateful for.*)

_____

_____

_____

9. On a scale from 1 – 10, indicate how you felt this week.

   Your self-confidence: _____
   Your energy level: _____
   Your happiness: _____
   Your drive and determination: _____
   Your health: _____
   Your wealth: _____

10. Indicate how much you are looking forward to next week, where you will learn about one method of finding the truth.

    ☐ I can hardly wait!
    ☐ I am really looking forward to it!
    ☐ I first will make sure I understood as much as possible in Part One..
    ☐ YES, I want MORE of it!

TIPS

> ➤ Be gentle with yourself if at first you don't understand everything. It will all be revealed as you go along. Promise!
> ➤ Drink lots of clean, natural water. Thinking and learning is an energy-intensive process. Water cleanses your system.
> ➤ Be more selective as to what you eat. "Bad" foods (those processed or high in sugar, salt, fat or empty carbohydrates; those with lots of preservatives, flavouring or colouring; those irradiated) will eventually deprive you of your divine energy. "Good" foods are unprocessed, not irradiated, grown organically and preferably come from close to where you live.
> ➤ Reduce your radio and TV consumption. If possible, eliminate it altogether for a while, and also make the decision to stay away from negative people and places.
> ➤ Affirm: "*Day by day, in every way, I am getting better and*

better." (This is the so-called "Coué-Affirmation". Émile Coué de Châtaigneraie (1857 – 1926) was a French psychologist and pharmacist who healed patients by simply instilling new belief systems.)

QUICK AND FUN EXERCISE

SMILE! Put on a HUGE grin and keep it on until you really have to laugh! Seriously! It not only strengthens your facial muscles, but also gives you a more healthy teint, and makes you feel great.

You can do this any time you feel down or depressed. Just do something silly and out of the ordinary. It will make you laugh about yourself and pave the way for more positive energies. See? It doesn't cost anything but your awareness and your claiming it.

NOTES

2

One Method of Finding the Truth

"One Method of finding the Truth" is the title of this second part. I hope you have understood and internalized the contents of the first part, so that you can now continue. If not or only partly, please wait or at least refer back often, as with your heightened understanding you will read more out of the each previous part.

This week it is important to memorise the offering of a strong **counter argument -or counter suggestion**- whenever you catch yourself thinking negatively, speaking negatively or doing something that is not to the benefit of all involved. By offering that counter suggestion, you are reversing the polarity of your thought. As thought is creative, you are also triggering a new chain of causation, and this changed thought will eventually have a **corresponding effect**.

You never fight anything you dislike. You are not offering resistance, because that leads to even more resistance. You are simply switching sides, and if you do this with the necessary persistence and trust, that new thought will also become habitual, then automatic, and finally imprinted on your Subconscious Mind. Once that has taken place, manifestation "just happens" and you no longer have "to think about it". Remember: manifestation is mostly subconscious!

Try to observe your thinking without judging it. Remove yourself from "the story" that you are acting out at that moment. Just observe it from a distance and offer the counter argument in case you notice something that caused resistance or that didn't feel good.

Your emotions/feelings are the key, because they govern your life. By learning to control your emotions, you learn to control your life. Remember: things and events just are. It's only us through our upbringing, education and therefore programming, that give them meaning in terms of "good" or "bad", "should" or "shouldn't". As it's only you doing it, it's also only you who has the power to change it – right here, right now.

So, **one** (there are others, as you will come to learn soon) method of finding the truth is by offering this strong counter suggestion, which the Subconscious Mind will act upon; but make that suggestion over and over again, because once is just not often enough to result in a tangible change in your life. Just like driving a car, walking as a toddler, or anything 'new', it's practice that makes perfect.

You will also learn that a thought directed with a particular purpose in mind will become **powerful**. Strong words, so once again: a thought directed with a particular purpose in mind will become **powerful**. It will become **full of power**. It will have strength, and it will start to live the very moment you bring in your emotions. Again, your emotions are your guidance system. Don't like how you feel? Well, then make the strong counter argument, or, if you don't know what it should look like, simply suggest 'freedom'. Yes, simply suggest 'freedom'! The Subconscious will also start turning that into reality.

Also important: in point 5 Charles Haanel says that ease and perfection depend entirely on the extent to which you cease to rely on your Conscious Mind. Why? Because as with actors, ease and perfection "happen" when they are in their element, lost in the acting, not thinking, wondering or analysing, but just 'being the character'. Thinking is the starting point, but with time you come to rely less and less on it, as your actions become habitual, automatic and then part of your very own Being.

This all points to the power of the Subconscious, and you are advised to understand this well, because especially in the beginning you are trying to analyse and dissect it all. That's perfectly normal, but you cannot stay in this mode if you want to effect real and easy change. It's a process of moving something from your Conscios Mind to your Subconscious Mind. The moment the Conscious Mind is freed, it has space for paying attention to something else, something new. You can imagine that this is only possible if things got moved out there first, because your Conscious Mind is not supposed to store all those things, but instead reason, analyse, combine, differentiate, etc.

ABOUT THE EXERCISE

This week you are dealing with **becoming aware of your thoughts**. Whereas in the previous week you dealt with physical control, now you are dealing with inhibiting thought, which is a conscious decision taken by yourself. To make it easier, simply focus your attention on the tip of your nose. By focussing you attention, you don't automatically think, because thinking has to be steered in a constructive, harmonious and systematic manner. By focussing on the tip of your nose, you are simply paying attention, nothing else.

Mastering this part and the exercise, too, prepares you for the following weeks, where you learn to relax both physically and mentally. First the control, then the order to relax. Please be diligent with this exercise! Also pay increasing attention to your sporting activities and your nutrition. Learning becomes much easier if the body is enriched with oxygen and the system doesn't have to use additional resources in order to maintain basic functions.

CHECKLIST

1. Please write down briefly where you caught yourself "in the moment" and offered the strong counter suggestion as explained in this part.

2. Indicate on a scale from 1-10 how you've felt this week.

	Previous Week	Now
Your self-confidence:	_____	_____
Your energy level:	_____	_____
Your happiness:	_____	_____
Your drive and determination:	_____	_____
Your health:	_____	_____
Your wealth:	_____	_____

3. Please write down the three most important things you've learnt in this part, in particular regarding the functions of the Subconscious.

   1. _____
   2. _____
   3. _____

4. Please write down which "unfavourable" situations you are now approaching with more awareness, insight, distance and sovereignty, in order to bring about another result.

   _____
   _____

5. Check those items that apply or that you have performed this week.

   ☐ Another person has changed its behaviour towards me in a positive way.
   ☐ I have changed my behaviour towards another person or situation.
   ☐ I have become more aware of my ability to actively control my thoughts.
   ☐ Before taking a decision, I stopped and asked myself what the outcome would be like.
   ☐ I have retrieved some experiences from the past and looked at them from an observer's perspective.
   ☐ This way I got new insights that I now regard as helpful.
   ☐ I have put more attention on conscious and deep breathing.
   ☐ I am catching myself more and more in the moment and observing my own thinking.
   ☐ I consciously took the decision to bring some unexpected joy into someone else's life.
   ☐ Before going to sleep I gave thanks for all the great things that happened that particular day.
   ☐ When getting up, I felt more energetic and optimistic.
   ☐ I have started thinking of or actually changing my diet to a more healthy one.

6. Which mode of operation has the responsibility of choice?

   _____

7. Please write down in which situations you are expressing negative emotions. Take your time to review them carefully, as much of that will be subconscious. **Note:** *Try to look beneath the surface and find out what the real reason might be for displaying such behaviour. Don't judge yourself as you go back in time. Just take note and observe.*

8. Write down how you felt when expressing these emotions and - if applicable - how it made the other person feel.

9. Write down what would change if you expressed yourself lovingly and with understanding instead. How would you feel then?

10. Indicate how much you are looking forward to next week and to finding out how thoughts become things.

    ☐ I can hardly wait!
    ☐ I am really looking forward to it!
    ☐ I first will make sure I understood as much as possible in Part One..
    ☐ YES, I want MORE of it!

RECOMMENDED READING

📖 Neale Donald Walsch's book series, "*Conversations with God*", is an eye-opener when it comes to identifying your thought patterns. Much conventional wisdom is questioned, and with it you arrive at a new outlook on your life and that of other people.

TIPS

- Counter suggestions or strong counter arguments are an indispensable part of finding the truth. They have to be repeated though, until they become as subconscious as the negative trait has become. We all learn by repetition, so keep them up and why not have fun with them? Expanding your consciousness shouldn't be serious and dull, but fun, irreverent and light-hearted.
- Be patient with yourself, because this is a radically new idea. Your persistent focus on what you desire will eventually bring it to you. But for that it needs to leave your Conscious Mind and be imprinted on the Subconscious Mind. As with everything, repetition makes it easier.
- Understand that it's all a process. Manifestation is not a jump from -say- 1 to 12, but a gradual progression, and the final step is from 11 to 12, and therefore totally normal and natural. It's the way nature intended things. Quantum leaps are possible, but are a strain to the system, and chances are that you won't be able to hold on to what you've gained.
- Reward yourself every single time you catch yourself in the moment, because then the positive outweighs the negative. Self-reward is very important, especially in the beginning.
- Develop an appreciation for the small, because the large is made up of many small things.

QUICK AND FUN EXERCISE

In the morning or whenever during the day, stand up, one arm up, index finger pointing towards the sky. Then jump up and down, saying/shouting "Yes, Yes, Yes! Today is going to be an awesome day! Yes, Yes, Yes!" You can also replace it with your own slogan, as long as it's positive and motivating. This is a nice and quick "charger". See for yourself the effect it has on you.

NOTES

3

Thoughts become Things

Now that you know that there is only one Consciousness that can think, you will learn that this can be moved to express itself in form by harmonious, systematic and constructive thoughts. Thoughts *become* things.

With every thought you activate receptors in your brain. Via the Vagus nerve they are sent down to the Solar Plexus, your inner sun and the seat of your habits. It's also your direct connection to the Universal Consciousness. As the Subconscious Mind doesn't argue but simply executes, it is of even greater importance to engage the "Watchman at the Gate", your Conscious Mind, in order to protect the Subconscious from any kind of negative, destructive thoughts. This is your obligation and responsibility. Observe yourself, filter, analyse, and let only the good things through, the things you'd like to have more of. In the beginning this requires your constant attention and awareness, but will show magnificent results if adhered to.

The quality, character and nature of our thoughts decide on how something is going to manifest. This means taking responsibility (the "ability to respond") for your thoughts, words and actions. No one has any power over you except for the power you allow them to have over you, and that is then a conscious decision with the **corresponding effects** on your life. So step by step you turn into a conscious co-creator, which is the purpose of your life.

You don't have to be afraid or need to worry. Everything will gradually unfold, and your increasing power to consciously co-create will become a growing source of joy and deep satisfaction in your life. As you are radiating more and more life (love) through your Solar Plexus, everything on the outside changes accordingly. Pay special attention to the small things while you are radiating life and love, compassion and understanding. You will become aware of the more subtle realms of energy, and this way an entirely new world opens up to you.

Here's a tip: turn this journey into fun ride. Laugh at your mistakes; enjoy catching yourself in the moment; have fun exploring your thoughts; ridicule your negative belief systems. Bring lightness - mind the word! - into your life, and everything becomes so much easier.

ABOUT THE EXERCISE

This week it's about **physical relaxation**. 'Tell' your muscles and nerves to relax. Calm down. Give up resistance. Breathe deeply. Practice this diligently and patiently. This way you also become so much more aware of your body, this beautiful vessel of yours. Take out all tension; this way you prepare yourself for the fourth part, where you let go of thoughts and relax mentally, too. Then you have an ideal foundation on which you can build with visualisation exercises that fire and empower your imagination, and therefore your ability to create mental images of the things you wish to manifest in your life.

CHECKLIST

1. Please write down what is meant by a "purposeful will" and why the Conscious Mind needs to be freed from your thoughts over and over again.

    _____
    _____
    _____
    _____
    _____
    _____

2. Indicate on a scale from 1-10 how you've felt this week.

	Previous Week	Now
Your self-confidence:	_____	_____
Your energy level:	_____	_____

Your happiness: _____ _____
Your drive and determination: _____ _____
Your health: _____ _____
Your wealth: _____ _____

3. Please write down the three most important things you've learnt from this part.

   1.
   2.
   3.

4. Please write down your understanding of the Solar Plexus and why it is so important that you let your light shine.

5. Check those items that apply or that you have performed this week.

   ☐ Another person has changed its behaviour towards me in a positive way.
   ☐ I have remained relaxed in an unfavourable situation and therefore changed its polarity from negative to neutral.
   ☐ I have consciously let my Light shine and expanded my Solar Plexus.
   ☐ I have engaged in relaxation exercises over and above the exercise of this week.
   ☐ Before taking a decision, I stopped and asked myself what the outcome would be like.
   ☐ I have retrieved another experience from the past and looked at it from an observer's perspective.
   ☐ I have noticed a change in my thinking when looking at it from a distance.
   ☐ I have once again placed more attention on conscious and deep breathing.
   ☐ I consciously took the decision to bring some unexpected joy into someone's life.
   ☐ Before going to sleep I gave thanks for all the great things that

happened that particular day.

☐ I can feel a rise in energy in my entire Being.

6. Please write down one thing that next week you will be placing particular attention on, in order to train your attention, awareness and imagination.

7. Write down any effect you can think of when your Solar Plexus is radiating and you are a "magnetic" person.

8. Write down what happens when you are no longer afraid of anything.

9. Write down what change you noticed within yourself while doing the exercise. How did it feel to totally relax and consciously inhibit all thought?

10. Indicate how much you are looking forward to next week and to finding out about the real "I", or your real "Self" and its infinite possibilities.

☐ I can hardly wait!
☐ I am really looking forward to it!
☐ I first will make sure I understood as much as possible in Part One..
☐ YES, I want MORE of it!

RECOMMENDED READING

📖 Bruce Lipton's „*The Biology of Belief*" shows us that we control our genes with our thoughts. Fascinating new insight into how we operate as humans.

NOTES

QUICK AND FUN EXERCISE

Grab your left ear with your right thumb and index finger, and your right ear with your left thumb and index finger. Now rub the ears with a good grip all around for about ten seconds. Repeat the same with your eyebrows, left to right, hands crossed. Then take one pinky (small finger) and rub the space between your nose and upper lip, while taking the other one to rub (left to right) the space just below your lower lip. Do that for 10 seconds too. This process is called "**de-switching**" and re-energizes you in just 30 seconds.

Camps Bay, South Africa. The mountain and the sea, storm clouds. Imagine being there now! Enjoy the view and may it help you get closer to your dreams, no matter whether they are of material nature like a nice home in a nice place, a great lifestyle, or something related to nature.

4

The Real „I"

Part Four deals with the real or true "Self", or the true "I". You will learn in this part that it is neither your bind nor your body. Both are mere tools for execution - instruments, that the "I" uses to express itself in form.

So what is this "I"? It is something spiritual, something intangible. As all Spirit is one Spirit, it is the **same in kind and quality as the Universal Consciousness** - the only difference being one of degree. This means that you have **unlimited resources** at your disposal, for that the Universal is Almighty, All-knowing and Omnipresent. What you can think, you can create. But it requires your mental appropriation, that "asking the question and getting ready to receive the answer". Without you staking that claim, no possession will ever come to you.

This is the essence of this part. Internalize it well, because understanding this "configuration" of your Being brings you in conscious cooperation with the Infinite Power.

As – in the spiritual realm – like attracts like, your wellbeing depends on the recognition of the wellbeing of the Whole. This means that your actions should never be selfish, but rather benefit all those involved. Nature never acts selfishly, but provides everything in abundance. As you are part of Nature, you ought to start doing the same - if you haven't done so already.

Remember that Positive Thinking is **just a first step** in the right direction. It's a means to an end. The end is the imprinting of that quality onto your Subconscious Mind, where execution and therefore manifestation takes place.

Self-denial doesn't get you anywhere. Accept yourself the way you are at present, because if you don't, nobody else will. But also acknowledge that you can always change what you don't like about yourself. Accept the status quo, yet at the same time embark on the process of reinventing yourself using the methods outlined in this course.

The acknowledgment of your connection to the Universal puts you in connection with it. Consciously become the channel through which the Universal can express itself. If you learn how to get your mind out of the way, the results are likely to be perfect.

You also learn in this part that the more you give, the more you will get. This is why it's so important to have **high, noble and great ideals**. The power you need in order to have those ideals comes through rest and silence, because only then are you able to concentrate, to focus on the things you desire, to reduce the distance between you and your wish, and to obtain the necessary detailed information you require on your path to manifestation.

It is **the feeling that gives life to the thought**, and this feeling comes through exercise, and therefore repetition. Feeling creates new neural pathways in your brain and causes your glands to release secretions. This has an immediate effect on your emotions, thus body, and will result in a new, albeit temporary, reality – just as some sad news would make you cry, or a joke would make you laugh, they are not meant to stay forever, but fade as quickly as they have appeared.

To recap: understand what this real "Self" is and what it means for your Being. This may be a true revelation, because perhaps for the first time ever you will become conscious of your **real power** and your true **divine potential**.

ABOUT THE EXERCISE

This week you **relax mentally**, removing any kind of negative thought. Hate, worry, anger, jealousy, sadness, envy, problems and disappointment have no place outside of your mind, so if you entertain them there, simply let them go. They aren't life-affirming, but life-negating. They rob you of your energy instead of increasing it. Also, by freeing yourself from such thoughts, you free yourself from the corresponding emotion. Subsequently, you will make space for the opposite kind of energy: love, compassion, understanding, friendship, joy, contentment, and sovereignty.

By mastering this exercise you can then control and therefore relax both your physical and mental being. This is the absolute foundation for all other exercises, so it's compulsory to master these first. If you still struggle with one of them, take your time and put in an extra effort - it's well worth it!

CHECKLIST

1. Please write down how distinguishing between cause and effect has made a difference in your life in this 4th week.

2. Indicate on a scale from 1-10 how you've felt this week.

	Previous Week	Now
Your self-confidence:	_____	_____
Your energy level:	_____	_____
Your happiness:	_____	_____
Your drive and determination:	_____	_____
Your health:	_____	_____
Your wealth:	_____	_____

3. Write down the three most important things you have learnt from this part, in particular how your understanding of your Oneness with all Existence feels physically and emotionally.

    1.
    2.
    3.

4. Write down why the Universal can act only through the Individual.

5. Write down three things that you are going to attract into your life using the affirmation "*I can be what I will to be*".

    1. _____
    2. _____
    3. _____

6. Check those items that apply or that you have performed this week.

    ☐ More than once I have become of the possibilities that are open to me.
    ☐ I have consciously let my light shine and expanded my Solar Plexus.
    ☐ I have consciously considered the effect my actions have on other people.
    ☐ I remain neutral and calm when I retrieve events from my past, knowing that they have occurred to teach me something in order to move ahead.
    ☐ Conscious and deep breathing is becoming part of my daily routine.
    ☐ I have become more and more aware of the beauty of and abundance in this world.
    ☐ I am thinking twice before swatting flies.
    ☐ My sense of courage and self-confidence is increasing steadily.
    ☐ I am making regular use of affirmations.
    ☐ I have begun or are expanding my vision board.

7. Write down why "emotions must be called upon to give feeling to the thought".

    _____
    _____
    _____

8. Write down why it is so important to finish something you have started.

    _____
    _____
    _____

9. This week I remember having consciously stilled my senses about _

times in order to gain insight into a particular matter.

10. Write down why it is important to be only interested in causes, not effects.

11. Indicate how much you are looking forward to next week and to finding out how awareness leads to success.

- [ ] I can hardly wait!
- [ ] I am really looking forward to it!
- [ ] I first will make sure I understood as much as possible in Part One..
- [ ] YES, I want MORE of it!

RECOMMENDED READING

- 📖 German MKS Student Michael Klenke recommends „*Kahuna Magic - The Science behind Miracles*" by Max Freedom Long as additional reading.
- 📖 "*Stillness Speaks*" is one of Eckart Tolle's books –a worthy read.

NOTES

TIP

> This is one of the most important parts of the Master Key System. Once you have really grasped and internalized that you are in essence Spirit, with infinite possibilities at your disposal, there is no more holding back from anything you've set your mind on. "The word is the name of God", I once read in an antique book. Remember this when you deal with the contents of Part Five.

5

Consciousness at the Centre of your Being

This fifth part marks the end of the first month of studying. Let us review it briefly and recall the most salient points.

Part One was about the understanding that there is only one Consciousness that can think, and when it thinks, it expresses itself in a myriad of ways. You are one with this one Consciousness. The only difference is of degree. You cannot express powers that you do not possess, but what you possess is undergoing constant change and can therefore be transformed and transmuted by the power of your thinking.

Part Two was about one method of finding the truth by means of a strong counter argument, often repeated, that you are offering in times of negative thinking, emotions or actions. It's mainly about your increased awareness of how you function, and how - once again - you can change this by the power of your thought. You always have a choice, no exception. As you are a holographic being, you notice many a thing, although it doesn't mean that you live out what you have become aware of. If you don't like what you perceive, you have to move to the "other side" in order to experience a distinctly different quality.

Part Three dealt with thoughts that become things. "Become", not "are". They just have to be held for long enough in your Conscious Mind. This way they turn habitual, then automatic and are then passed on to the storehouse of the Subconscious Mind, making space in your Conscious Mind for new thoughts, and subsequently things.

Your Conscious Mind decides over the quality of our thoughts, meaning: the type and quality of information that you pass on to the Subconscious. There, no further argumentation is taking place - everything is accepted as fact. Wrong thinking leads to wrong results, with the obvious negative consequences for your being. With the "Watchman at the Gate" fully alert, only positive thoughts are being passed on, while the negative ones are being denied access and therefore cannot manifest themselves as they did before. It also dealt with the Solar Plexus, your inner sun, and that this sun needs to radiate life. You have learnt how to activate your Solar Plexus, and this is of paramount importance, as it is the gateway to your heart chakra.

Part Four was about your real "I" (or Self), which is of a spiritual nature. This means it has infinite resources at its disposal. All you have to do is lay a claim, or rather: ask the question. It motivates you, and pushes you to think and do harder. It uses both the mind and the body as instruments, or tools, in order to experience itself. Your senses only indicate to you what has already happened and what you are receptive for. Once again, if you don't like what you see, change your thinking. This way you change the physical makeup of your brain and thus your nervous system, too. The outer world is a world of effects. The inner world is a world of causes. The inner world is the practical world, and it is you, by the power of your thought, who learns to become a master of your own life.

These four weeks you will have spent ample time with the exercises. If not, stop right here and review your reason for not conducting the exercises. You may also want to start with Part One again, until you have mastered the exercises and therefore yourself. Remember, this is not about mere intellectual satisfaction, but about learning something new, and then applying it on daily basis, turning you into a new Being. How else could desirable change be effected if there is no one laying claim to that change?

In this fifth part you learn that the Conscious Mind can direct the Subconscious Mind, as the latter doesn't engage at all in analysis or argumentation – it merely executes. The Conscious Mind, limited as it is, has a very important role, the role of the aforementioned "**Watchman at the Gate**". Once understood and used accordingly, you will remove fate, destiny or pure chance from your life, which is now governed by your understanding of law. Not man-made law, mind you, but Universal Law.

You learn in this part that you are a result of past thinking, your own or that of other people. You have been influenced by the outside without any or much question or analysis. This is now coming to an end, as your Conscious Mind is on full alert, carefully weighing up which information is being passed on to the Subconscious, and which one is rejected at the door.

You learn that you become what you think today. You also learn that the Law of Attraction doesn't bring to you what you desire but what you are today. Otherwise you wouldn't be able to perceive it with your senses.

Charles Haanel advises us to be very careful and selective with regards to the material we use to build our mental house. Only the best material should be used. For you this means only to think the best thoughts possible. So pay good attention to how you spend your life, what media you expose yourself to, how you react to negative news, and - most importantly - how much time you spend entertaining constructive rather than destructive thoughts.

You learn that all possessions are the result of an accumulative mental attitude. Today more than yesterday, is the motto. That the resulting wealth will quickly exceed your own needs goes without saying, so you will pass it on, enriching others and once again be enriched in the process, but again: first you have to give it!

After the first four weeks were spent with mental and physical control and relaxation, you are now starting with the first **visualization** exercises. Remember only to select the best mind material if you wish to manifest the best results in the outer world. You now have a strong foundation for the weeks to come, as you will learn to visualize better and better, and also learn to concentrate more on what you wish to manifest in life.

Finally, your conscious connection with the Almighty enables you more and more to express strength, courage and faith. You are in the process of discovering the correct mechanism to be used in order to bring about the desired results. This way you become conscious co-creators, and create this Universe with every single breath you take!

ABOUT THE EXERCISE

This week you recall a past event of which you have pleasant memories. The details will come to you easily, as people tend to fade out negative memories and only recall the good ones. So take your time keeping these images in your mind. What you are doing here is the first step towards any goal: you create something intangible by the power of your mind and thought, and step by step transform them into tangible values. But first you need to learn to create such mental images and steadily hold them in your mind until you can proceed.

CHECKLIST

1. Please write down briefly in which way you have practically demonstrated your conscious awareness of yourself or life in general in this week.

   _____
   _____
   _____
   _____

2. Indicate on a scale from 1-10 how you've felt this week.

	Previous Week	Now
Your self-confidence:	_____	_____
Your energy level:	_____	_____
Your happiness:	_____	_____
Your drive and determination:	_____	_____
Your health:	_____	_____
Your wealth:	_____	_____

3. Write down the three most important things you have learnt from this part:

   1. _____
   2. _____
   3. _____

4. Write down what it means to you to have an accumulative attitude of mind.

   _____
   _____
   _____

5. Please write down how the recognition of your relation to your home, business and social environment shows in daily life and which benefit you derive from it.

6. Check those items that apply or that you have performed this week.

    - [ ] I have become more aware of the smaller things in life, the details.
    - [ ] I have used my authority to repress or refuse an undesirable trait or characteristic.
    - [ ] I have been ever more relaxed with regards to myself and my environment.
    - [ ] I have spent time in nature, connecting with plants and animals.
    - [ ] I have become more aware of the inheritance that is waiting for my claim.
    - [ ] My breathing has become more conscious, slow, deep and rhythmic.
    - [ ] I have become more ware of my real "Self" and the infinite opportunities available to me.
    - [ ] My physical fitness is getting on par with my mental fitness.
    - [ ] I have been consciously grateful for every experience I have made.

7. Write down what the "Law of Attraction" brings to you today.

8. Write down what it takes to acquire a mental attitude of the best kind.

9. Write down what is necessary to gain access to the domain of mind and spirit. Hint: Look up and internalize point 15 if you don't have the answer right away.

TIPS

- Develop an attitude of gratitude! This is one of the unspoken secrets of the Master Key System, in which you will find no word of thanks or gratitude. It's therefore for you to develop and nurture. You cannot be grateful for something that hasn't happened, so by giving thanks, you reduce the distance between you and your dream to zero. You also do this by affirmations formed in the present tense, "I AM...".
- Do something out of the ordinary every day. Push your own limits and have fun doing so. Learn a few words of a new language every day, or take a course in something you're interested in. Mingle with happy and successful people. Up your exercise routine –or start one!

QUICK AND FUN EXERCISE

Go and hug a tree or the next person or pet that you come past. Smile and say "thank you!" Just do it and see what happens. Again, extraordinary deeds yield extraordinary results!

NOTES

6

From Awareness to Success

You become aware of something when you pay attention to it. Attention and concentration are of paramount importance, because it is your attention that attracts further energy. Your intention governs your attention, and your attention results in you becoming more conscious. With this you will be able to focus (or concentrate) on any given thing, issue or topic. And as you concentrate, you once again become more aware and conscious, and a higher level of consciousness is nothing but a more fine-tuned human being, able to perceive so much more than before, when it was rough, uneducated, uncivilised and not making use of its divine potential.

When you focus, you automatically exclude other thoughts[1], which means that you won't become conscious of those things. Let me repeat: if you keep concentrating your thoughts on one particular thing, you exclude other thoughts, just as much as what you become conscious of shows up in the world outside. While you are reading this, you aren't paying attention to your watch or the clouds outside. No attention, no awareness, no consciousness, no benefit. It really is as simple as that.

A thought is energy. A concentrated thought is concentrated energy. Your thinking has to be harmonious, systematic and constructive. It must be in alignment with the forward movement of the Universe, which means that

---

[1] In Quantum Physics, they call this 'collapsing the wave function', as light behaves like a wave when not observed, but like a particle when observed. As soon as it gets observed, it takes on distinct properties, to the exclusion of others. The same applies to your thought.

sender and receiver must be on the same wavelength. Remember that there is no lack or limitation in Nature or the Universe. Abundance is apparent everywhere. But unless you acknowledge and internalize that, it cannot manifest in your life. You see lack and limitation? You will get MORE lack and limitation. You see abundance? Well, then you will get MORE abundance. It depends entirely on how YOU see things.

Remember that as long as you have to think about something, you aren't "it" yet. You "are" something once it has left the conscious realm and is performed or executed instinctively. The Subconscious is the place of manifestation, not your brain. So, once again: through repetition you can influence the Subconscious Mind, which executes flawlessly. You need to practice over and over again, because practice makes perfect. And perfection depends entirely on the degree to which the issue at hand has left your Conscious Mind. An exercise that takes time, awareness and focus, but which will reward you abundantly in return.

ABOUT THE EXERCISE

After recalling a past event in last week's exercise, this one is about a photo, preferably your own. While looking at it, you become aware of the details. Then you cover it and recall those details from memory. This exercise serves to train the mind to recall things that have been stored, like any kind of positive thought or emotion or detail about a goal or purpose or ideal you have in mind. The more details you can pick up, the more conscious you become, and the higher the benefit you derive.

Remember: the more details you pick up, the more information you absorb. Later on, this increased information intake leads to a **recognition of patterns**. You can see when and how things are repeating themselves. Out of that comes certainty, then centeredness, then peace of mind, then intelligent decisions. This sequence is very important to understand and internalise, because it keeps repeating itself all everywhere in existence.

CHECKLIST

1. Please write down why "aspiration, desire and harmonious relations constantly and persistently maintained will accomplish results."

2. Why are "erroneous and fixed ideas" our greatest hindrances?

3. Indicate on a scale from 1-10 how you've felt this week.

	Previous Week	Now
Your self-confidence:	_____	_____
Your energy level:	_____	_____
Your happiness:	_____	_____
Your drive and determination:	_____	_____
Your health:	_____	_____
Your wealth:	_____	_____

4. Please write down the three most important things you have learnt from this part.

   1.
   2.
   3.

5. Please write down why it is paramount that you do the exercises on a regular basis.

6. Write down why thought has to be constructive and creative.

7. Check those items that apply or that you have performed this week.

   ☐ I have noticed someone in my vicinity to change his/her behaviour towards me.
   ☐ An 'unexpected' present was given to me.
   ☐ I have become more and more aware of my thinking and how I

        am expressing it in words.
- [ ] I have recognized at least once that I am not part of the story that is playing itself out in front of me.
- [ ] My breathing is becoming slower, deeper and more rhythmic.
- [ ] I have become aware of the mental world I live in.
- [ ] I have become more aware of what I eat and drink.
- [ ] My physical fitness is improving.
- [ ] I have reduced my TV, radio and newspaper "consumption", or at least become more selective.

8. "As thy faith is, so be it unto thee", bears the stamp of scientific test. Explain.

9. Explain what is meant by "the brain is an embryonic world".

10. Explain what is meant by "The Temple of the living God".

11. Please indicate how much you are looking forward to learning more about the power of your imagination.

- [ ] I can hardly wait!
- [ ] I am really looking forward to it!
- [ ] I first will make sure I understood as much as possible in Part One..
- [ ] YES, I want MORE of it!

QUICK AND FUN EXERCISE

Nice little yoga exercise: Sit upright. Stretch out your arms to the side, palms up; bend your lower arms so that your thumb touches your shoulder/back while the other four fingers rest on your clavicle/chest. Now breathe in **through your nose** and turn your upper body to the left, breathe out and turn to the right. Then breathe in again as you turn to the left, and out again as you turn to the right. Start very slowly so that it's comfortable; later on you can increase the breathing and therefore the turning speed. As a variation, breathe in and out upon each turn. This cleanses your lymphatic system and makes you feel very energetic.

Watch the video with Maya Fiennes at: http://youtu.be/4Mzu04kH9BY

NOTES

7

The Power of your Imagination

Imagination, the ability to create mental images, is the connecting link between you and the fulfilment of your dream or desire. By imagining things you are tapping into the Universal. You are creating something out of nothing – out of 'no thing', out of spirit! Obviously, this takes more than just a few random thoughts and its related images. As mentioned before, you will have to keep that image in your mind and ensure that doubt gets eliminated completely. Once you've set your goal, you will stick to it. Otherwise you are setting yourself up for failure. If this isn't clear to you, please look up Part 4:12 again.

When you use your imagination, you are becoming a channel, through which the Universal expresses itself. When you use it positively and harmoniously, you are in alignment with Creation. When you use it negatively, you are just as creative, but you will attract the corresponding effects into your life. There is no escaping from this fact.

Did you know that you cannot imagine anything that doesn't exist? Or the other way round, whatever you can think of and picture in your mind, you can also create and manifest. Isn't that amazing? Obviously, you are bound to certain limitations, but at its base, those limitations are mere mental constructs themselves. Personally, I believe there is method to it, because it's only through those constraints that creation is possible in the first place, and reliable on top of it.

All that is required is an ideal, followed by focussed thought, which gives rise to more details and its corresponding feelings. With the feelings comes verbalisation and strong and decisive action, ultimately leading to the expected result.

The language is the Universe is feelings, they say. This is why it's so important to imbue your thoughts with feelings, because without them they remain cold and without the necessary life force. Feelings are hormonal releases into your body, so when you feel, a corresponding biochemical reaction is taking place on the physical plane.

You may be among those who haven't learned to ask, to claim, to assert themselves. You have to ask in order to receive. With the Master Key System, you learn to ask, all the while readying yourself for the answer. This readying is the faith that you deserve to receive it, and that you are good enough to receive. There's a devious programming in many people, that makes them believe that they aren't good enough or deserving of the nice stuff, be it material, health or in relationships. Out with that! From now on you will actively pursue your dream, calling it forth from the first image in your mind into a denser and low-frequency realm of first emotion, then matter.

Your *question* (or wish, desire, prayer, concentration, ...), however, is not directed at mum, dad, the boss or someone else, but the Universal Consciousness. You are asking the part within yourself that already exists as pure potential, but now using the mechanism, you are essentially taking it out of this realm, changing it into something tangible. This is the creative process of getting material things through creative visualization. Remember, it takes time and persistence, and - as Charles Haanel said - "a boundless amount of self-confidence".

As with all other things, the more (intelligently) you train, the better you become, so with time you can create bigger things, bigger ideals, more colourful and lavish and extravagant pictures. The previously unimaginable now becomes almost routine, and you, as a human being, have lifted yourself onto a new level. As you become more fine-tuned, and by using the right words and doing the right things, step by step your life will turn into symphony of harmony, beauty, order, love, health and wealth. It's obviousuly not because of your thinking alone, but because of courageous action you are taking, as you keep the end result firmly in mind.

Once again, it's your predominant mental attitude that - quite literally - matters, and not the random thought or idea you have every now and then. If you then understand that this process is not haphazard but systematic, it will be even easier to engage, and make your dreams come true.

While we are at it, let's have a quick look at the word "system". One of its properties is that it accomplishes much with very little energetic input. This way it becomes self-sustainable. This is the reason why your thinking has to become systematic, because then you won't need much energy in order to effect anything. And if you understand the sequence, you can turn it into a system for your own and the benefit of others. The sequence is as follows:

1. Idealization – a goal that you are going to accomplish
2. Visualization – the corresponding images in your mind
3. Feeling – the act of treating it as it if had already happened, leading to hormonal releases and therefore biochemical changes in your body.
4. Speaking / Verbalization
5. Doing / Action

+ Belief / Faith
+ Trust
= Knowledge

First we need an **ideal**. This ideal takes shape in form of **mental images**. Then you need to give details to these images and **feel right into them**. You need to treat our ideal as an *already accomplished fact*. This is done by the use of feelings. Once you have allowed this thought to germinate in silence – undisturbed – and gather strength (more on that in Part Eight and Nine), you can come out in the open and **communicate** it. The **actions** will then follow, and this last step is the crucial one, for nothing happens without a corresponding action. No matter how much you visualize, love and feel good, you have to get off your butt, especially if you desire material riches.

While initially we didn't *know* that we could have this, we needed *belief* and *faith*. *Trust* was a logical result of treating the ideal as an already accomplished fact. And out of that *trust* in the process, understanding that Creation is subject to law, came *knowledge* and *confidence*. And once you *know*, you no longer need to *believe* (in this ideal).

Isn't it amazing to see how the functioning of your imagination can be steered so easily and be repeated whenever the need arises? Once you've found this mechanism of truthful thinking, you will be able to tap into the Universal at your leisure. Then there is no turning back anymore, and you will be filled with drive and determination to create the best version of yourself ever.

Part Seven is the logical continuation of what you've learned in Parts One to Six. Now that you know how this mechanism functions, apply it right away. Once again it requires repetition, but this repetition creates habits and influences the subconscious.

ABOUT THE EXERCISE

This week deals with a mental manipulation of a situation that has taken place for real. So you recall your meeting a good friend, and in your mind you tell him or her something and wait for the reaction. Remember, this all takes place in your imagination, nowhere else. But this is an important exercise as it trains your imagination and allows you to see someone or something else with different eyes. Make that person laugh and smile and be full of energy and joy. This way you develop a consciousness for it and will subsequently see a corresponding effect in the world outside. But for now it's less about manifestation and more about the training of your imagination - the ability to change your thinking and therefore your corresponding mental images.

CHECKLIST

6. Please write down how you can attract those things into your life that you require for expressing your Highest Good.

   _____
   _____
   _____
   _____
   _____
   _____

7. Indicate on a scale from 1-10 how you've felt this week.

	Previous Week	Now
Your self-confidence:	_____	_____
Your energy level:	_____	_____
Your happiness:	_____	_____
Your drive and determination:	_____	_____

Your health: _____   _____
Your wealth: _____   _____

8. Write down the four steps towards materialization.

    1.
    2.
    3.
    4.

9. Write down why the image you have created must be clear and clean-cut.

10. Feeling, thought and will correlate to each other like desire, expectation and demand. Explain.

11. Check those items that apply or that you have performed this week.

    ☐ I have thought about new things.
    ☐ My thinking has become clearer and more clean-cut.
    ☐ I have notched up my dreams and expectations.
    ☐ I have become aware of the fact that the only difference between myself and the Universe is one of degree.
    ☐ My sleep is solid and sound.
    ☐ I woke up in the morning feeling relaxed and refreshed.
    ☐ I have made regular use of affirmations, directing my thinking in the right direction.
    ☐ I have become increasingly aware of all the beautiful things around me.

12. Explain what is meant by the "Great Architect of the Universe".

13. Why must something be established firmly in your inner world before it can take an outward manifestation?

14. What is it that you have to find if you want money, power, health and abundance?

15. Meditate for a while on the word "imagination" and try to absorb its very essence.

QUICK AND FUN EXERCISE

Next time you meet a friend, look at him or her closely and find out all the facial or behavioural characteristics you have in common. Let him/her do the same with you. Take joy in all your new discoveries!

NOTES

8

The Value of Truthful Thinking

"The value of truthful thinking" is the title of this eighth part, and is taking you to the end of your second month of studying. If you are still showing the same kind of diligence and motivation, I congratulate you!

In this part you learn about truthful thinking. If your thinking is not full of truth, how do you think the results look like? Finding out what truth really is, was already the subject of previous parts. Here you learn that your life is the result of law, not of chance, fate, destiny or caprice. This once again fills you with gratitude, and a warm feeling emerges. You are the one making constant use of these laws, but now consciously, constructively and systematically. You are the individualization of the Universal. We all are. All we have to do to create a wonderful, healthy, wealthy and loving life is to understand the laws and apply them.

Small thoughts and self-denial won't get you anywhere, because they return to you exactly what you've sent out. You're here on this planet to experience yourself, to create ever more greater versions of yourself, to improve on previous versions and incarnations and learn your true potential and how to tap into it.

The same applies to big thoughts (a topic of a later part of the Master Key System). If they are in alignment, read: conscious, systematic and constructive, they too will manifest in accordance with their own nature. Truthful thoughts are those that have principle; those that can sustain themselves from within of their own being. Remember: false thinking leads to destruction, wheras truthful thinking leads to construction.

False thinking is therefore void of principle, as the Bad cannot exist with out the Good, but the Good can pretty well exist without the Bad. It only needs the Bad for definition purposes, but not for its own growth and existence. Therefore, please pay good attention to this quote by George Matthew Adams:

"Learn to keep the door shut, keep out of your mind, out of your office, and out of your world, every element that seeks admittance with no definite helpful end in view."

As long as you are an apprentice, you will not always notice the detrimental thoughts that constantly seek access to your Conscious Mind. Unfriendly vibrations is what you could also call them. Do not fight them, because resistance causes more resistance. Let them go. Change their polarity. Move over to the other side! THAT's where your solution and salvation lies. Tell apart the real from the unreal. Do not let yourself be blinded by effects. Change the cause; the effect will change accordingly.

Thinking that isn't truthful also has the habit of robbing you of energy. Truthful thinking on the other hand provides you with energy. There you can see how one kind of thinking destroys and the other kind of thinking creates. Choose wisely!

Remember that not all thoughts manifest instantly. Thinking is the precursor of manifestation, but thoughts alone, without feeling and the necessary amplification, lead to nothing. It's your mental attitude that counts, not a thought of love, health and wealth entertained every now and then. Persistence and belief and trust are the keywords.

So all errors are just errors of ignorance. This part teaches you to recognize the truth and to make use of it. This makes it so powerful, so useful, so in alignment with the forward movement of the Universe. Truth is what has principle. Polarity, read: duality, is an integral part of it. This is why it's so important to look at things without judgment and without attaching any negative value to it. Things just are, and the quicker you can absorb this wisdom, the more negativity and all its corresponding effects will vanish from your life.

ABOUT THE EXERCISE

Truthful thinking can only show where Cause and Effect are known. This is why I recommend you reading and absorbing the wisdom of the Kybalion, so that you develop a keen understanding of the Hermetic Principles.

Once you know that each effect is just a cause for another effect - and that in both directions, you can trace back something to its point of origin. This is the purpose of the exercise of Part Eight.

First of all you learn to trace back the battleship to its origin. You trace a material object back to its origin, only to end up with thought. Thought and therefore spirit is the ultimate reality, the ultimate cause.

You also learn to look closely, to peer beneath the surface. Only then will you become aware of the finer details, in this case the workings of a battleship. A rough observation would never reveal such details. So you learn to pay better attention, because the rare facts are the valuable ones, not what everybody else knows.

You also learn that this battleship is only powerful because of so many people, read: so many thoughts, words and actions. It is powerful in the negative sense, because it brings death and destruction. And many people play a role in this game, without thinking, not knowing what causes they set for themselves in the process by having others doing the thinking for them.

So, you learn to trace back a material object to its point of origin; to look closely and become appreciative of the finer details; to understand that there is strength in numbers, IF those numbers are organized. Chaos has no power, but order has. And order is systematic, and a system achieves much with relatively little energetic input.

Use this exercise to become aware of the complexity of the end result. Become aware of all the steps that are necessary for something to be effected, for it to manifest. It's that kind of detailed, truthful thinking that will lead you to success. And in its final essence, it teaches you to stop thinking destructive thoughts and thus stop creating destructive things like this battleship.

So you see, life is a lot more complex than you think, but with time and the necessary mental effort you will find it increasingly easy to get to the core of a thing without much analysis. Here, as with everywhere else, practice makes perfect.

CHECKLIST

1. Explain the meaning of service. Write down why it is important that our actions have to be to the benefit of the greatest number.

   _____
   _____
   _____

2. Indicate on a scale from 1-10 how you've felt this week.

	Previous Week	Now
Your self-confidence:	_____	_____
Your energy level:	_____	_____
Your happiness:	_____	_____
Your drive and determination:	_____	_____
Your health:	_____	_____
Your wealth:	_____	_____

3. Write down why all mistakes are merely mistakes of ignorance.

   _____
   _____

4. Write down why the ideal that you have created must be held in your mind for a prolonged period of time.

   _____
   _____

5. Write down why it is so important to recognize the difference between cause and effect.

   _____
   _____

6. Check those items that apply or that you have performed this week.

- [ ] I am the one more and more in control of my own thinking.
- [ ] I am feeling energetic and full of drive and determination
- [ ] I am able to tell cause and effect apart.
- [ ] I've learned that my own thinking is the ultimate cause.
- [ ] I've recognized complex patterns and can trace them back to their point of origin.
- [ ] I've realized more and more how nature provides everything in abundance.
- [ ] I've continued practicing deep and rhythmic breathing.
- [ ] I've found it easier to imagine big things and that they are attainable for me.
- [ ] I am affirming that I am good enough to attain them and that I am deserving of them.
- [ ] My own gratitude is increasingly reflected in the gratitude of other people towards me.

7. Write down how you can cultivate your imagination.

8. Look up point 17 and write it down verbatim.

9. What does it mean to you to live in Unity with all things and all life?

RECOMMENDED READING

📖 The "Ringing Cedars" series of the Taiga recluse *Anastasia* by Vladimir Megré is a wonderful extension of the topic "Unity with all life". It conveys a very different style of living and of the restoration of the natural beauty of Planet Earth. An excerpt: "*After reading Anastasia thousands of people have quit their jobs! Why? Because...The Ringing Cedars Series contains some of the most important revelations to appear in thousands of years of human history—so significant, they are changing the course of our destiny and rocking scientific and religious circles to the core. Powerful, myth-shattering messages in these books reveal profound wisdom grounded in ancient knowledge, expose suppressed secrets and hidden historical fact and offer a whole new paradigm for our planet's future.*"

📖 There is an antique book called "*The art of getting material things through creative visualization*" by Ophiel. In it you learn about the "sphere of availability", which explains why some dreams come true and others don't. This is very important to know in your quest to become a mastermind.

TIP

➤ Make a habit of randomly picking out objects and observing them in detail. The "battleship" exercise was a start, but this skill of discovering the not so obvious has to be practiced and honed, too, in order to be of practical use to you.

NOTES

9

Action as the Blossom of Thought

Part Nine is about "Acttion as the Blossom of Thought". Why that? Because it's nice to think positively, make affirmations, create new images, visualize, etc., but without action it simply never enters the realm of energy densification, also called "matter". Action is the flower, the true unfoldment of natural beauty, of harmony, of love. It is the effect of various causes that you have set in motion, that you have consciously introduced into your life.

Matter is high-density energy, and high-density means that a large amount of it is available. Its availability to you depends entirely on your mental appropriation, on your will, as well as the discipline and understanding of the mechanism. That said, it should be remembered that the actual effort diminishes with time, as you have more strength and power than just a few weeks ago. It also means that because of your personal magnetism and radiance, other people will feel attracted to you and support you in your efforts. This means less effort, more liberation, and even more motivation.

By the way, how are the cold showers doing? Smelled a flower today or listened to the singing of the birds? Turned in a circle and fired yourself up? No? You think it's too silly? Well, I still do it, because it's a great way to start the day. Our empowerment and enabling does not take place outside of nature. Quite the opposite, in fact. It is more inclusive of our true nature, of our connection with all that nourishes and sustains us. This includes the affirmation. "*I am whole, perfect, strong, powerful, loving, harmonious and happy.*" Wholeness and perfection are about Health, strength and power about Wealth, and the other two about Love. And if you are all six, then your are automatically happy, because with health, wealth and love, there is nothing that can be added to your cup.

In this part we learn to change circumstances or conditions using the Law of Growth. We keep the desired condition in our Conscious Mind, while excluding all other competing or doubting thoughts. In this part it is the affirmation:

"I am whole, perfect, strong, powerful, loving, harmonious and happy."

This is a statement in strict accordance with the truth and works wonders reinventing yourself, so make a habit of it.

You learn that the mechanism, through which you accomplish anything you desire, is the way you think. Nature produces everything in abundance, and your non-participation is only because of our erroneous thinking. As you change this, you connect to the Source and cause it to shower you abundantly - always in strict accordance with the nature and quality of your thought!

You then turn into a conscious channel, through which the Universal expresses itself. But this doesn't mean that something flows through you. You aren't the flow. The Universal is the flow. You just have to open the sleuth gates or doors, otherwise the channel dries up. As soon as it's open, the channel fulfils its predestined role and derives a benefit from it, while also benefiting others. This is what Charles Haanel meant when he said that **what benefits one, must benefit all**.

This also means that you don't have to worry about the "water", because all this is already present in the realm of the Universal. Just make sure that you are the right conductor and open to the flow. The rest is just as automatic as your blood circulation, your nervous and your digestive system. All these are subconscious processes and demonstrate the real power of the Subconscious Mind, while you as a person are moving from a lower to a higher level of evolution.

Your knowledge of the truth makes all doubt go up in flames, and you will tackle new projects with courage, determination and trust – all defining traits of great minds. The world is your oyster and it does everything for you. It works for you, informs you, motivates you, excites you, because it is just as much an expression of the Universal Consciousness as everything else.

This is the truth, and you will notice a change in resonance as you increase your own rate of vibration. These are like energies, and they are well-meaning energies to boot. No favouritism here, just law. You think rightfully and harmoniously, and your life will reflect this new attitude of yours. This is called a closed resonance system, and you remember one of the main properties of a system, right? I explained this a few weeks ago.

So the path will be opened up to you, and even there you will find rocks lining the way, but as you have learnt how to think truthfully, rather than being a victim of circumstance, you will learn how to remove those rocks and clear the path.

This new resonance also means that there are other energies or "chunks of consciousness" that you will no longer feel comfortable with. This is normal and will continue for the rest of your life. This is all good. You have to say goodbye to old energies, thought patterns and habits, and make space for new ones.

ABOUT THE EXERCISE

Last week you were tracing something material back to its spiritual origin. This week you do the exact opposite: you are sowing the seed, watching how its roots penetrate the mineral realm and make use of its energies. After a period of non-disturbance, it breaks through the surface and stretches towards the sun in order to fulfil its intended purpose.

What does it mean?

1. A sunflower seed will turn into a sunflower, not an apple tree. A seed of love will therefore turn into much bigger love.

2. Once sown, leave it undisturbed. It needs to gather energy and strength from the lower realms first. Don't go out trumpeting your idea around to other people. Be silent, think it over, add details, give it emotions.

3. Everything material has a spiritual origin, and just as the battleship can be traced back to the ideas of a few people and the irresponsibility of the many. The final sunflower can be traced back to its seed, which has been thought up by the Great Architect of the Universe. Once a sunflower, it has fulfilled its purpose of providing food and joy. New seeds are then carrying on with the same purpose of becoming sunflowers, but better and more perfect versions than the previous one.

So the seed is your thought. It has to remain in darkness and silence first, before it is strong enough to face the forces of the elements. But once it is, it will reach its pinnacle as a sunflower. Haanel urges us to seek solitude and silence. Still your senses, away from the hustle and bustle of modern life. Seek insight and inspiration. Think new thoughts, let them gather strength, and then go all out to fulfil them, to make them come true.

Please take the necessary time for this part and this exercise.

CHECKLIST

1. Explain why we must treat our wish as an already accomplished fact and therefore reduce the "distance" between us and our ideal.

2. Indicate on a scale from 1-10 how you've felt this week.

	Previous Week	Now
Your self-confidence:	_____	_____
Your energy level:	_____	_____
Your happiness:	_____	_____
Your drive and determination:	_____	_____
Your health:	_____	_____
Your wealth:	_____	_____

3. Which law are you invoking in order to make manifest your desired circumstances?

4. Write down why it is so important to know the Truth.

5. Explain the principle behind the statement that a positive thought will push aside a negative one.

6. Check those items that apply or that you have performed this week.

    ☐ My behaviour towards other people has become increasingly friendly, compassionate and understanding.
    ☐ I am regarding my own behaviour and that of others in a neutral manner.
    ☐ I am catching myself in the moment and am offering a strong counter suggestion in case of an erroneous thought.
    ☐ I am more and more capable of directing my thought towards my Solar Plexus and make it radiate and expand.
    ☐ I acknowledge more and more that life just wants to express itself and that even the "negative" things or events are merely there to teach me something
    ☐ I am becoming more and more conscious of the effects of my deep and rhythmic breathing.
    ☐ I take cold showers.
    ☐ I motivate myself in order to accomplish the goals I have set for myself.

7. Please look up the affirmation of point 11 and write it down verbatim.

8. Why is »I am whole, perfect, strong, powerful, loving, harmonious and happy« an exact scientific statement?

9. Allocate the terms of the above affirmation to one of these groups:

    1. Health:
    2. Wealth:
    3. Love:

10. Please look up and internalize point 30. Then write down how the change in your mental attitude has been demonstrated in your life in the past two months.

11. What does the "Law of Attraction" bring to you and why?

12. Meditate on the inner and outer planets of our Solar System and put their qualities and characteristics in relation to your own evolutionary journey, the chakra system and your Master Key study.

RECOMMENDED READING

📖 James Allen's *"As a Man thinketh"*, as well as Napoleon Hill's *"Think and Grow Rich"* are wonderful supplementary reads.

NOTES

10

Life in Harmony with Natural Law

When we talk about Natural Laws, we talk about the Law of Growth, the Law of Attraction, the Law of Cause and Effect, etc. On this note I would once again like to remind you of the *Kybalion*, in which the 7 Hermetic Principles are explained in great, albeit pretty abstract detail.

It is one thing to know about those laws, yet another to make conscious use them until they have become second nature. Once this has happened, you are no longer controlled by and at the whim of others, but a conscious co-creator, a powerful human being that lives in harmony with itself and its environment. If the phrase "controlled by others" leaves you with an uneasy feeling, then rightly so. But this is exactly what you get if you don't do your own thinking. In that case you get what others have thought up for you, and trust me, it's hardly what *you* wanted, but in all cases what *they* wanted. Does that make you feel good? Is it really serving you? The answer in most cases and upon close inspection is 'No'.

So focus your attention inward and find the source of all Power. This is done by your mental appropriation. What you appropriate is a better understanding of how life works and what the underlying natural laws are. You see how the circle closes? Knowledge then becomes power, but power depends upon use, so you bringing yourself into alignment with such laws and their application in life will make you a very powerful being.

You learn in this part to control our emotions and feelings, because if you don't, they exert control over you. And once they control you, things are likely to happen that you later regret. You learn to use your emotions and feelings in order to give life to the thought. Thoughts impregnated with feelings develop life – or vital force – because feelings are life already, so new life stems from preexisting life. It is important to understand that persistence – read: repetition – plays a crucial role here. Why? Because it means amplification, and amplification leads to densification and materialization. It's the thinking of the same thought over and over again, imbued with feelings over and over again, so that it can gain life and manifest accordingly.

Take good note of point 14, when Charles Haanel quotes the Great Teacher, who said: "*It is not I that doth the works, but the Father that dwelleth in me, He doth the work*". He continues: "*We must take exactly the same position; we can do nothing to assist in the manifestation, we simply comply with the law, and the All-originating Mind will bring about the result.*" So it is our compliance with the law that makes our life; our noncompliance would break it and "*bring about disease and possibly death*".

You know by now that Nature produces abundantly. Now we learn that all Wealth comes from Power, but not from the abuse of it, but our conscious appropriation of it, to the benefit of all involved. Power diminishes through non-use, and without Power, no Wealth.

You learn that "*possessions are only of value as they confer power. Events are significant only as they affect power; all things represent certain forms and degrees of power.*" So, something that doesn't confer power is of no value. Spend some time over this quote or section - it's right at the beginning of Part Two - because it helps you understand that your actions must empower others and therefore be of benefit to them.

Now, after 9 weeks, you will have made progress to such an extent that the "*You*" is no longer comparable to the "*You*" from just a few weeks ago. The coming weeks will again deepen your understanding and you will gain more confidence and courage to move beyond the intellectual understanding and into the realm of action, fearless, well-executed action.

More and more often will you look at the same things with different eyes and recognize the Grand Scheme of Creation behind it, with you as a conscious co-creator. More and more often will you make use of your knowledge and understanding and transform, transmute and transcend whatever you deem necessary.

ABOUT THE EXERCISE

The exercise of Part Ten contains certain occult symbols. So it's not so much about drawing some imaginary lines on the wall in front of you, but about understanding what is taking place there.

The horizontal line is the first individualization of the point.

The vertical line indicates a first change in dimension.

The square represents the male element, structured, methodical, limiting.

The circle represents the female element, the infinite that gives birth to all, but needs to be limited by the male.

The point in the circle is not only the symbol of our Sun, but also the Individualization (yourself) with the Infinite. By drawing the point nearer to you, it will soon be One with the Circle, so by appropriating the Individual, you are becoming one with the Infinite, and are able to give it any colour or shade you like. All this is done through the power of your thought.

On another level you are creating a cone by pulling the dot closer to you, and a cone is a vortex, a transformation of energy, either a compression or an expansion, depending on the direction of rotation. So you see, this is not about some silly lines, but about a much deeper meaning behind it. Once again, the level of your awareness determines your consciousness and therefore your use and benefit.

CHECKLIST

1. Explain why abundance is a Natural Law of the Universe. Write down the implications for your own life.

2. Indicate on a scale from 1-10 how you've felt this week.

	Previous Week	Now
Your self-confidence:	_____	_____
Your energy level:	_____	_____
Your happiness:	_____	_____
Your drive and determination:	_____	_____
Your health:	_____	_____
Your wealth:	_____	_____

3. What distinguishes a successful from a common person with regards to Cause and Effect?

4. Write down why possessions are only of value as they confer power and results only of significance as they affect power.

5. Please review point 8 and spend some time meditating on its meaning. Become aware of the top-down movement of intelligence that enables and empowers the lower realms as they are touched by the higher realms.

6. "Thought is the connection between the Infinite and the Finite." Why is that and what are the implications for your own life?

7. Check those items that apply or that you have performed this week

    ☐ I'm becoming more aware of how things or persons enrich my life.
    ☐ I'm becoming more aware of how I enrich other people's lives.

- [ ] Undesirable conditions are manifesting less and less in my life as I am becoming aware of their true nature and their lack of principle and truth.
- [ ] My increasingly positive vibes are being noticed by other people.
- [ ] More and more people approach me for help or assistance.
- [ ] My physical fitness is improving all the time. I live a healthy life.
- [ ] My media consumption is being reduced significantly. Instead, I look up places in nature where I can be alone with my thoughts.
- [ ] I have understood why my thinking has to be in alignment with Natural Laws. This shows in my daily life.
- [ ] I see things with different eyes, look at the same external effect yet see a completely different thing.

8. Why does creative thinking have to be harmonious, and what brings it about?

9. Explain why thought has to be in harmony with the creative principle of Nature.

10. Write down the meaning of Polarization and how it manifests in your daily life.

RECOMMENDED READING

- 📖 Michael Talbot's "*The Holographic Universe*" reveals so much more about how the universe works, how all this information is stored and how we can access it. Not an easy read, but very worth the while.
- 📖 On that topic, Peter Tompkins' and Christopher Bird's book "*The Secret Life of Plants*" tells us about those beings that give us so much joy and that are providing us with much needed life energy.

NOTES

EXERCISES

1. Redraw this Nautilus shell while meditating on its meaning.

2. Look up "Fibonacci" or "Golden Mean", and relate it to the above.

11

Inductive Reasoning

"Inductive Reasoning" is the title of this 11th part, to which I welcome you warmly and with peace and blessings. It is the continuation of all that you have learnt in this third month, so no abating of this divine knowledge.

Induction is what happens when you compare individual cases in order to find a common denominator which gives rise to them all. What does that mean? It means that if you recognize the common denominator, you know that there is no chance or luck involved anymore, but law. This way you come from belief to knowledge and from knowledge to the truth. It will not escape you that belief or faith serves a purpose, and this is to lead you to knowledge and therefore the truth. And once you know, you don't have to believe anymore - at least not in this thing. So "belief" can be termed "the proof of the things yet unseen", and with each new ideal, you are starting off with belief and faith, but ultimately have to arrive at knowledge and truth. No other belief is of any value.

To know the truth also means to be conscious of your power and strength. This only grows through appropriation – exercise and repetition. If you aren't making use of your power, it will soon dwindle and disappear. This is as true in the spiritual realm as it is in the physical. If you've been engaging in physical exercise, you will know exactly what I mean.

It may be the first time ever that you become consciously aware of the central role your feeling of time plays and your appropriate verbal expression of it, because here we aren't dealing with linear time but with 'Zero Time', concurrency, simultaneousness. You recognize the importance of expressing yourself in the present tense, "I am", and not in any future or relative form like "I will" or "I could" or "Someday..." or "Soon", but "Now" and "I am". If you express yourself in the present tense, you are reducing the distance between you and your desire or wish or dream to zero, and therefore helping it to manifest rather than keep pushing it in front of you.

"I am" is a very powerful statement, and remember that this thought and verbalization is a vibration that will resonate with like vibrations. Now spend a few moments on how you verbalize your dreams. Because that's how you think about them. And that's how they will manifest - or rather, not manifest, because you keep pushing them in front of you, without ever reaching them. You know, someday I will be rich and health and happy. Rubbish!

I AM, I AM, I AM! Healthy, wealthy and happy!

Haanel says that "we are thus thinking on the plane of the absolute and eliminating all consideration of conditions or limitation and are planting a seed which, if left undisturbed, will finally germinate into external fruition."

He also says that no single statement or human formula will ever state the completeness of truth, so it has to be expressed in different ways in different times. In this part he is doing just that.

ABOUT THE EXERCISE

The aforementioned quote from the Bible is the focus of this week's exercise. You have to believe that something has already been given to you. Then all doubt will disappear and leave you filled with hopeful expectation, courage, trust and motivation to take further action. The only limitation is the one you place on yourself, but as you have learned in Part Four that your true essence is spiritual and therefore unlimited, you will find it much easier to break through your habitual thinking and dream up bigger things and make them happen in a structured and methodical manner. The knowledge of your power will lead you to the application of this power and then to the manifestation of this power.

Remember: Faith is not a shadow, but a substance, »*the substance of things hoped for, the evidence of things not seen*«.

CHECKLIST

1. Explain "Inductive Reasoning" and why it is important to find a

scientific base for your assumptions.

2. Indicate on a scale from 1-10 how you've felt this week.

	Previous Week	Now
Your self-confidence:	_____	_____
Your energy level:	_____	_____
Your happiness:	_____	_____
Your drive and determination:	_____	_____
Your health:	_____	_____
Your wealth:	_____	_____

3. Why do we have to believe that our desire or wish has already accomplished in order for it to materialize or manifest?

4. Write down what the creative power of thought consists of.

5. What does it mean in your life to think in "absolute" terms?

6. "Wisdom starts with logical thinking". Why is that so?

7. Explain why there is no more room for doubt once you have created an Ideal.

8. Write down where in this week you have made use of Inductive Reasoning.

9. Check those items that apply or that you have performed this week.

- [ ] I am engaging more and more in constructive thinking rather than just having random thoughts.
- [ ] I am becoming increasingly aware of the connections between things that are superficially disconnected.
- [ ] I am affirming that I am not the story that is playing itself out in front of me, nor that it is my story.
- [ ] I am becoming aware that in those moments I am merely having thoughts, and erroneous ones at that, but that I am not really thinking, for thinking is conscious, systematic, and constructive.
- [ ] I find more and more joy in life.
- [ ] People in my environment notice the changes that are occurring in my life. I am taking this as a sign of support and encouragement.

RECOMMENDED READING

- „*Stalking the Wild Pendulum*" by the late Itzhak Bentov is a highly recommended book on the mechanics of consciousness and a theoretical explanation of the Universe. There it is also explained what technically happens when we meditate.

NOTES

12

Understanding the Spiritual Nature of Thought

Welcome to this 12th Part of the Master Key System. It brings you to the end of the third month and therefore half-time in your studies. Congratulations for studying so diligently and persistently!

This week you are dealing with "Understanding the Spiritual Nature of Thought". This is nothing really new to you anymore, because you've taken cognizance of it in the first parts already.

In order to accomplish anything at all, you must create an ideal. What else

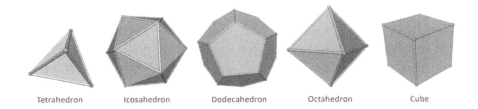

Tetrahedron   Icosahedron   Dodecahedron   Octahedron   Cube

should our attention be directed at if not an ideal? This ideal, **always** formulated in the present tense "I AM …", already exists by the power of your imagination, albeit in the very fine and subtle form of mental images. All you are doing now is to adjust its shape and form, its external manifestation. In other words: you are stepping it down in frequency and increasing its density.

On a physical level, atoms vibrate faster than molecules, and they vibrate faster than crystal lattices, the first form of visible physical manifestation[1]. The origin is always on a spiritual plane by means of thought and its subsequent transformation to a physical manifestation, wherever this is desired. Just remember that you are a spiritual being, so you won't find lasting satisfaction in physical objects, but in happiness and harmony. This is what you are really after, but have been blinded to believe that to enrich yourself with physical objects is the primary reason for your existence. Wrong! They are means, but not ends.

So once you've created your ideal, it's your task to visualize it, meaning: enrich it with details. The more detailed your ideal, the more information, thus consciousness, is available to you, pointing you to ideas and concepts that aid the final manifestation. Again, having an ideal is nice, but it needs details.

Take a car, for instance: It carries you from A to B in the most comfortable manner, but how many thoughts (details) have gone into this car before it could become a car and therefore take shape the way you see it?

Take your body: it enables you to do the most magnificent things, but how many thoughts did it take to create this marvellous vessel of yours? Please treat it accordingly, will you!

It is you alone who decides on how the ideal looks like and how many details you add to it. It is your belief in yourself as a creator that makes this creation grand, or shabby. The details surface in the Silence, in meditation and concentration. This is when you get inspired. You are literally getting "breathed into", which is what "inspired" means. The Universal Breath of Life flows into you, with all its abundance and with pure Love as the underlying principle of existence. This is what constitutes the flow, while you are making the channel available and therefore controllable.

Demand governs supply, and if you don't ask and don't believe and don't trust, how can you ever receive? "*Ask and it is given*", is the title of a book by Esther Hicks, and this boils it all down to one single sentence. But you, now being in week 12, know how to ask and why you should ask, too. You know about the ideal, about the visualization, about the imbuing of thoughts with feelings, of trust, a harmonious language, moral, mental and physical cleanliness, of 'Zero Time' and of your Oneness with the Universal and its limitless forms of expression.

---

1 Physical manifestation is based on the Five Platonic Solids. This is another subject worthy of investigation and contemplation.

The ideal you create is yours. It doesn't have anything to do with other people or circumstances. It is the grandest version of your current ability to think and imagine. Remember Part Nine, where we were talking about leaving the seed undisturbed. So create your Ideal and hold it in your consciousness, so that its roots can develop and gather strength. This is a prerequisite for the final manifestation, which is why it is so important to keep silent about those things and to work with them in your mind only. When the time is come to go out in the open, you will, but by then your Ideal will be strong enough to weather the elements, including any negative comments from other people, or your own residual doubt.

Quick question: are you still enjoying your cold showers? How is the meat consumption doing? Reduced it or gotten off it altogether? How about your physical exercise? Twelve weeks of it should have made you a lot fitter. If not, well, it's yours when you want it badly enough. Until them make the most with what you've got and enjoy what it gives you!

ABOUT THE EXERCISE

This week the exercise is about your conscious cooperation with the Almighty, your recognition and appreciation of the unlimited possibilities it provides. But for their provision we need the tools, and the tools are truthful thinking, idealization, visualization, feeling, love, trust, courage and boundless self-confidence! Take your time to obtain an exact understanding of how you relate to the Universal. Without comprehension, no brain cells, and without brain cells, no nerve cells, and without nerve cells, no perception in the outer world. 'As above, so below.'[2]

Also take some time to remember how much time you spend with TV, newspapers, radio, etc. absorbing effects rather than setting causes, and internalising other people's thinking rather than creating your own thoughts.

Understand that meditation is a wonderful way to stretch time. In it you will have the opportunity to experience so much more than the actual physical time would afford you. Meditation is an inner world journey, while your waking consciousness is an outer world journey. In meditation you absorb and receive, whereas in your normal world you simply consume. Think that over.

---

[2] These words circulate throughout occult and magical circles, and they come from Hermetic texts. The concept was first laid out in The Emerald Tablet of Hermes Trismegistus, in the words "That which is Below corresponds to that which is Above, and that which is Above, corresponds to that which is Below, to accomplish the miracles of the One Thing". Source: Wikipedia.org

CHECKLIST

1. Write down your current Ideal and how this will benefit others over and above benefitting yourself.

   _____
   _____
   _____
   _____
   _____

2. Indicate on a scale from 1-10 how you've felt this week.

	Previous Week	Now
Your self-confidence:	_____	_____
Your energy level:	_____	_____
Your happiness:	_____	_____
Your drive and determination:	_____	_____
Your health:	_____	_____
Your wealth:	_____	_____

3. Explain the role of visualization in the creation of your Ideal.

   _____
   _____
   _____

4. Why is it so important that you hold on to your Ideal once created?

   _____
   _____
   _____

5. Why can the Infinite not be influenced or changed?

   _____
   _____
   _____

6. Check those items that apply or that you have performed this week

- [ ] I have become more aware of the importance of ideals in my life.
- [ ] I am relaxed. Nothing negative affects me anymore. I am sovereign.
- [ ] My ideals stand tall and firm.
- [ ] I am laughing about myself and my own mistakes.
- [ ] I recognize the Universal ("God") in everything.
- [ ] I feel more and more connected with what we call "God".
- [ ] I am taking cold showers and enjoy its effects on my body.
- [ ] I am healthy.
- [ ] I have been directing more of my attention towards wealth and abundance, irrespective of its outward manifestation.

7. "The Law of Attraction is just another name for Love". Why is that so?

8. Explain why only good alone can confer permanent power?.

9. The intention governs the attention. What is meant by this and how do you understand it?

10. Write down the scientific explanation why Silence puts you in touch with the Omnipotent.

NOTES

13

The Law of Cause and Effect

The receiving of this part marks the beginning of the second half of your studies. Once again, congratulations! One of the main changes from now on is in the exercises. After they've appealed to your logical mind for most of the first half, they will now focus more on the right side of your brain, strengthening your concentration skills, even on rather abstract topics like "insight" or "harmony".

Content-wise you will continue to become aware of your connection to the Omnipotent, the Universal Intelligence, and how to consciously tap into it.

This will enable you to take a far more active role in reality creation. The resulting gratitude will lead to more and more, and you can't but share it with all those you come in touch with. Abundance in all relations awaits you!

In earlier parts you've already heard about the Law of Cause and Effect, but now you learn that wealth isn't primarily what you are striving for, but harmony and happiness. You are a spiritual being and cannot find lasting satisfaction in anything material. Material possessions are just means to an end and should never be mistaken for anything else. That said, they still provide pockets of joy and allow for gratitude, having attained something that may have been a dream for a very long time. At the same time don't every forget that spirit is the only thing that lasts.

The Law of Cause and Effect is one of the seven Hermetic Principles. It explains that for every effect there is a definite cause. This cause we need to track down in case of disharmonious effects, because once we know the cause, we can make the strong counter suggestion, thus moving over to the other side where different qualities exist.

It is important to understand that the solution for every problem is ALWAYS on the other side. Energy follows attention, so no matter how much we dislike something, as long as we keep thinking about it, as long as we fail to transform, transmute or transcend it, it will cling to us and so will its effects.

Charles Haanel says that a happy thought cannot exist in an unhappy consciousness, and we are using the aforementioned Hermetic Principles to create such happy consciousness and to establish it for good. Remember, manifestation is subconscious, so it requires a disciplined, determined and prolonged effort as far as the counter argument is concerned.

The Law of Cause and Effect will bring certainty to your life, where previously there was chance, fate and caprice, at a time when you didn't know of these natural laws. Inductive Reasoning and the careful observation of the lesser known details, together with the knowledge of cause and effect will draw any secret from anything you put your mind to.

Finally, please pay special attention to point 23, where Charles Haanel says: *"Thought is a spiritual activity and is therefore creative, but make no mistake; thought will create nothing unless it is consciously, systematically, and constructively directed; and herein is the difference between idle thinking, which is simply a dissipation of effort, and constructive thinking, which means practically unlimited achievement."*

ABOUT THE EXERCISE

In this part you learn anew that it is your recognition of the Omnipotent and our ability to align yourself with it that is the basis for all attainment. This can only happen in the Silence, and therefore this week's task is to go into the Silence and become deeply aware of your unity with the Omnipotent.

You see that the exercises are taking on a different quality. They require you opening to your inside world, so that both inspiration and intuition come to you easily. Take your time and see if you can establish this connection and to let things flow into you that you didn't deem possible only a short while ago. Remember that everything exists 'in solution', as pure potential. It is you who has to make the claim, to ask the question. Do it! There is nothing to lose! Set new causes in motion and keep this unity with the Omnipotent in mind until it has become an integral part of yourself. Support and enhance this by looking at your daily life with different eyes, and come to realize how everything is connected, even though it doesn't appear obvious at first.

CHECKLIST

1. Write down the role harmony and happiness play in your life.

2. Indicate on a scale from 1-10 how you've felt this week.

	Previous Week	Now
Your self-confidence:	_____	_____
Your energy level:	_____	_____
Your happiness:	_____	_____
Your drive and determination:	_____	_____
Your health:	_____	_____
Your wealth:	_____	_____

3. Explain why we have to give before we can receive.

4. Thought has to be conscious, systematic and constructive. Why?

5. It's the unusual observations and facts that have the highest value. What does this mean for your own life?

6. Check those items that apply or that you have performed this week:

- [ ] I am becoming increasingly conscious about the causes that I am setting in motion.
- [ ] I understand that each thought is a cause with a corresponding effect.
- [ ] I recognise that my taking notice of negative things doesn't mean that I bring those things to life myself, but that I am merely observing.
- [ ] Every day I am filling my lungs with fresh air and am enjoying the Prana (life force) that I am absorbing this way.
- [ ] Pets are reacting positively differently towards me.
- [ ] I am increasingly grateful for all creation..
- [ ] I am feeling more and more like a conscious co-creator of my reality.
- [ ] I am actively pursuing my dreams, turning them into reality though idealisation, visualisation, verbalization and action.
- [ ] I am becoming increasingly conscious of my own wealth and how to attract more into my life.

7. What kind of consciousness needs to be present, so that joy and happiness can express themselves?

8. Explain what it means to you personally that "knowledge doesn't apply itself".

9. You are part of the Whole. Write down how you have applied this knowledge in your life by means of a practical demonstration.

RECOMMENDED READING

- *"The Kybalion"* by the Three Initiates is a free download on www.masterkeysystem.tv. It explains the seven Hermetic Principles in great detail, including the Law of Cause and Effect. It is compulsory reading, if at first not easily understood in all its aspects.

NOTES

"True, without falsehood, certain and most true, that which is above is the same as that which is below, and that which is below is the same as that which is above, for the performance of miracles of the One Thing. And as all things are from the One, by the meditation of One, so all things have their birth from this One Thing by adaptation. The Sun is its Father, the Moon its Mother, the Wind carries it in its belly, its nurse is the Earth. This is the Father of all perfection, or consummation of the whole world. Its power is integrating, if it be turned into earth.

You shall separate the earth from the fire, the subtle from the gross, suavely, and with great ingenuity and skill. Your skilful work ascends from earth to heaven and descends to earth again, and receives the power of the superiors and of the inferiors. So thou hast the glory of the whole world--therefore let all obscurity flee from thee. This is the strong force of all forces, overcoming every subtle and penetrating every solid thing. So the world was created. Hence all were wonderful adaptations, of which this is the manner. Therefore I am called Hermes Trismegistus having the three parts of the philosophy of the whole world. What I have to tell is completed concerning the Operation of the Sun."

OPENING OF THE EMERALD TABLETS,
BY HERMES TRISMEGISTOS

14

The Discipline of Thinking

Discipline has been with you on a daily basis, otherwise you wouldn't have made it this far. Disciplined thinking, however, is something completely different. Here your imagination merges with inductive reasoning and deep concentration, in order to get method and structure into any of your undertakings.

After 13 weeks I trust you have observed some significant changes in your thinking and mental attitude in general. This means you will have discovered both sense and senselessness in many of your thoughts and behavioural patterns, and have taken the necessary steps to move over to the other side.

Talking of which, please write down all the things that have changed in these past three months. Review your checklist in general and check the progress you have made. If you aren't happy with it, you know what to do: redouble your efforts; review past chapters; undergo an honest self-analysis as to why this could happen. If you are happy with the progress you've made, all the better - you are to be congratulated!

In this 14th part you learn that whatever you pay attention to, will gain more life energy. This isn't really news to you anymore. However, the same principle also applies in reverse. This means that whatever you withdraw our attention from, you deny its life energy (vital force), and just as a flower slowly wilts once cut off, so will bad or negative energies wilt when you cut them off at the root. This will require a certain amount of awareness, but chances are that you are already in possession of this level of awareness. From now on you will only pay attention to what you want more of and withdraw attention from anything you want less of. Simple and straight-forward, and something that will revisit you many a time in the coming months and years in your quest for a higher level of consciousness.

Charles Haanel once said in an interview that it doesn't require us to tear down the old; it only requires us to build up the new. The old will then gradually disappear anyway. David Lynch, a renowned movie director, once answered to a question from the audience: "Just because you've become conscious of it doesn't mean you got less of it." And this is precisely the point. We keep focussing on the negative and then wonder why it doesn't disappear. We keep focussing on lack and limitation, and are surprised to find more of that manifest in our lives. Weird, isn't it?

Remember well that there is no one judging you. No one gives a hoot about what you think, how disciplined and harmonious and constructive your thinking is. But **you** should! If you are still locked in old patterns or belief systems, understand that you don't have to analyse them to death. A simple recognition is often enough in order to move over to the other pole with its opposing qualities. As always, it's a matter of exercise, read: repetition. Practice makes perfect.

An example: if you feel depressed, the solution lies in focussing on power, strength, joy and abundance. All these are mental tasks. Nothing physical is required, nor does it cost any money. This focus will draw in additional energies of like quality - the Law of Correspondence is in operation here. Of course, you can assist your mental work with natural means, in this case lavender, or… pasta. Both are known to enhance moods.

Spend some time imagining what it means to be powerful, strong, joyful and with enough of everything. You will quickly become more aware of the details on how to accomplish this in real life. You could jump under a cold shower to "shock" your system, engage in physical exercise, eat some foods that are known to raise your mood or just go into the Silence and recall Part Four, where you have learnt that your True "I" is of spiritual nature and therefore cannot be anything but perfect, and that any error is an error of ignorance. So pay attention to the details that have escaped you so far. Again, it takes discipline in thinking, which is what you are learning in this part.

I have made a habit of offering the strong counter argument in situations where I know that they aren't getting me anywhere. This doesn't mean that those thoughts will not come again - they do - but with every counter argument I am moving closer to the truth, closer to the other pole with its different qualities. Should I be in a bad mood (false thinking), then I know that if I go to bed and sleep (read; turn off my Conscious Mind and allow the all-knowing Subconscious Mind to take over), and when I wake up it looks much better.

I have also made a habit of giving thanks when I go to bed. I briefly review the day and pick out everything that I could be grateful for. I always find at least 4-5 things, and with that energy and programming I fall asleep. Also, remember the affirmation from Part Nine. Say it out loud a few times, too, when you go to bed, because this also influences your Subconscious Mind.

This 14th part once again reminds you that the Universal provides everything in abundance, but that it is you who has to stake the claim, ask the question, pray, meditate, concentrate or whatever you prefer calling it. The result is the same, as long as you don't search for the Omnipotent outside yourself, but rather find it where it truly rests: in the intelligence of every single cell of your body.

ABOUT THE EXERCISE

Well, it will shower you with harmony, that's for sure, because every day, for 20-30 minutes it is your task to concentrate on harmony. In this deep concentration become aware of everything harmonious: your life, the growth of plants, the life of galaxies, the alignment of the planets around the sun, the love of a mother and a father towards their child, the change in ebb and flow, your breathing, your blood circulation, the movement of the clouds across the sky, the cycles of day and night, etc. These were just off the top of my head; there is just so much more you can and will become aware of with a little effort.

This exercise is of particular importance if you aren't feeling well mentally, or physically. Its sole aim is to bring you back into alignment, a place of peace and .... harmony. Picture the intelligence of every single cell of your body. Picture it going to fulfil its predetermined task with utter precision. Picture a perfect end result, one of beauty, order, flow and harmony.

So wherever you turn, nothing but harmony, nothing but a pure symphony of beauty and perfection. Your concentrated effort leads to an increase in consciousness, and said harmony will show up more and more in your life. That's the purpose of this exercise, which you will conduct with the necessary discipline and diligence.

CHECKLIST

1. Write down why denying undesirable conditions is as effective as concentrating on desirable conditions.

   _____
   _____
   _____

2. Indicate on a scale from 1-10 how you've felt this week.

	Previous Week	Now
Your self-confidence:	_____	_____
Your energy level:	_____	_____
Your happiness:	_____	_____
Your drive and determination:	_____	_____
Your health:	_____	_____
Your wealth:	_____	_____

3. Write down all the negative aspects of your life you are now going to deny the vital force they require.

   _____
   _____
   _____
   _____
   _____

4. The Individual is merely a distribution channel. What does this meant to you in practical terms?

   _____
   _____
   _____

5. Things have no origin, nor permanence, nor reality. Why is that so?

   _____
   _____

6. Check those items that apply or that you have performed this week.

- [ ] I have left point 3 of this checklist empty, because otherwise I would have paid attention to something I wanted to stop paying attention to.
- [ ] My thinking is disciplined and I take great joy in doing the exercises.
- [ ] I find it easier and easier to identify the ultimate cause of every effect.
- [ ] I catch myself in moments where I think negatively and make a strong counter argument in order to change the polarity and thus quality of the thought.
- [ ] I am understanding and patient towards myself and my learning progress.
- [ ] I am increasingly seeking places of solitude and inspiration.
- [ ] I am affirming strength and health for myself and follow them up with specific actions.
- [ ] I recognize the Love of the Universe and am feeling this love manifest more and more in my life.
- [ ] I am motivated and keen to gain new insights and make new experiences. I love life!

7. *"Man's life is an image of his thoughts."* What does this mean to you in terms of what we call "the future"?

8. Explain the role of the Subconscious in manifesting and materializing your dreams and desires.

9. Write down why it is so important that no one interferes in the decisions you have made.

INSPIRATION

"Abundance with iris" by Yuko Halada,
http://www.zenshodo.com/gallery.htm

NOTES

15

Conscious Co-Operation with Natural Law

This week it's about our conscious cooperation with Natural Laws. I trust you have mastered last week's exercise, as it is prerequisite for tackling this one.

You may ask yourself, "How can I cooperate with the Omnipotent?" Isn't it nice to know that it's really very simple? You do this by getting into alignment and thus harmony with Natural Laws. In plain English: it means by thinking, speaking and acting harmoniously, systematically and constructively. As this leads to corresponding feelings, you are establishing a conscious connection to the Omnipotent. This way you enrich your life and the lives of those you come in touch with. All this, as you know by now, is being effected by going into the Silence.

We learn in this part that thought has to be filled with love in order to gain the necessary vital force. Once again: the thought needs to be imbued and thus filled with the emotion of love in order to gain life. Love should accompany any of your thoughts, words and deeds.

Charles Haanel said that we need to let go of the things that don't serve us anymore, and that we must accept those that do serve us. This means we need to open up and become receptive to the new, and close up and finish off with the old. How is that being done? By your mental appropriation and by repetition. Practice makes perfect, but that practice first and foremost takes place in your mind.

When you refuse to let go of what doesn't serve you anymore and reject to accept that which does serve you, how can a life on higher planes become available to you? You cannot continue doing and thinking the same things you did before, while expecting a drastic change in your conditions. Disharmony and obstacles disappear the moment you open up, get into the flow, and accept that which serves you.

As a consequence, your speech and actions need to correspond with this change in mind-set and deepening of our understanding. Only clear and concise words that have principle and are therefore in accordance with the truth should leave your mouth. Only actions that benefit others as much as they benefit you should be taken. As this is a journey and not an overnight thing, be gentle to yourself, but keep doing it, as the results are nothing short of amazing.

Clarity in thought will lead to clarity in action, and where there is clarity, there is no confusion. Clear action, combined with love-infused thoughts will bring about a corresponding result. Keep this in mind whenever you are about to say or do something. It also helps you keep the faith as your are following your mission.

Speech is a 'programme'. Only a few of us are really aware of what they are saying. Luckily, this changes and has been changing with you studying the Master Key System, because your choice of words becomes more and more conscious and thus selective, once again with the corresponding results. Pay good attention, because your ears indicate to you what you have just thought and brought into the world by the use of words.

ABOUT THE EXERCISE

This week's task is to concentrate on insight. This exercise helps you understand that the knowledge about the creative power of thought doesn't mean that you possess the art of thinking. Knowledge needs to be applied in order to be of benefit, and your understanding of this well lead to well-thought-of actions that serve others and as a result serve you. By doing this you enter into a conscious cooperation with the Omnipotent. Having insight is a rare skill, but even that skill can be developed and honed.

If you find it difficult to conduct this exercise, I suggest you reread those sections of Part Fifteen again that explain what Insight is and what it is good for.

CHECKLIST

1. Write down why all Laws are working in your favour.

2. Indicate on a scale from 1-10 how you've felt this week.

	Previous Week	Now
Your self-confidence:	_____	_____
Your energy level:	_____	_____
Your happiness:	_____	_____
Your drive and determination:	_____	_____
Your health:	_____	_____
Your wealth:	_____	_____

3. Write down, what difficulties, disharmony and obstacles are indicating to us.

4. Why can we only receive what we give?

5. Why are all conditions and expectations that come to us to our benefit?

6. "There is no principle of error." What does this mean?

7. Explain the importance of Insight in your life.

8. What are the invisible and invincible powers that will objectify themselves?

9. Write down why a harmonious language is so important for the realization of our goals.

10. Please revisit verses 9-11 of this part and meditate on them for a while.

11. Check those items that apply or that you have performed this week.

    - [ ] I am paying more and more attention to a harmonious verbal expression.
    - [ ] I am consciously placing myself in harmony with the great eternal forces.
    - [ ] I notice my environment is changing as I am changing.
    - [ ] I still enjoy cold showers.
    - [ ] My physical fitness is improving.
    - [ ] Deep and rhythmic breathing has become part of my daily routine.
    - [ ] An increasingly complete picture of the Universe and my role in it is forming in my mind.
    - [ ] I can easily let go of old things that don't serve me anymore.

12. Explain the Law of Compensation

RECOMMENDED READING

📖 Walter Russell wrote a wonderful book, called "*The Secret of Light*". It sheds more light on God, Creation, yourself, your life and your reality.

NOTES

16

Creating Scientifically True Ideals

This week you are dealing with the creation of scientifically true ideals. It took me a while to really understand what this means, but certainly not right away when I first read this chapter.

Scientifically true ideals are first and foremost those that are in alignment with the Omnipotent; ideals that are harmonious, constructive and systematic. There is another aspect to it, though: Growth is always gradual. Step by step our skills and faculties improve, and as we get stronger we are able to make bigger things happen. So scientifically true ideals are also those that we are currently able to make happen. This is why it is important to set goals that are within your "Sphere of Availability". This phrase helps you understand why some things come to you with more ease than others. Using the creative power of thought you can expand this sphere and therefore attract other things into your life. Remember: you cannot express powers that you do not possess.

You learn in this part about the Law of Sevens, and that everything is being governed by periods or rhythms. The better you understand those rhythms, the better you can adjust yourself when a particular quality is showing. Far more importantly, though, you can use the power of our mind to convert those energies into their polar opposites the moment you notice them having a negative influence on yourself.

In this regard I would like to draw your attention to the Maya Calendar (www.lucita.net), which helps you understand some much larger rhythms or evolutionary stages. It also provides a tool that allows you to realign yourself with the intent of creation. Why is that necessary? Because the calendar governs our consciousness, and as our calendar is linear yet consciousness develops exponentially, it doesn't serve us as a guideline for the development of our consciousness. The Tzol'kin calendar of the Mayas is stepping down some very large evolutionary cycles and enables us to absorb and internalise the quality that each day has. Our own calendar is void of any information regarding the day quality. Make it a habit to tune into the Tzol'kin and observe your consciousness expand and develop accordingly. You will appreciate that the two are in perfect alignment with each other, because the qualities you become aware of using the Tzol'kin are the same you are developing with the Master Key System.

The bottom line of this is profound yet simple; it's **always** about the recognition of patterns. This pattern recognition can only take place if we open our mind and let more information flow in. Out of that pattern recognition comes certainty, because we know when what is recurring. This helps us become centred. Centeredness leads to peace of mind. And out of peace of mind inevitably leads to intelligent decisions. And those again lead to the perpetuation of life and your existence on higher planes.

Wealth is an offspring of labour, but this labour doesn't have to be of the manual kind. You learn in this part that wealth is merely a means in order to serve others and as a result serve ourselves. As much leads to more, the more you give, the more you will receive, and that allows you to give even more and therefore receive even more. Do you now see and understand how you will get rich? Your wealth and richness is the **result** of enriching others, because where else would the money come from if not from them? And why should they part with their money if they don't derive a benefit from your service? See, this sheds a rather different light on things material, doesn't it?

In closing: our increase in mental, emotional and physical strength will allow you to create even more and greater things. You see that the small stuff works, like finding free parking. Then you try something a little bigger and more complex and more daring. Your attempt in making that happen results in further growth, and once you are on that level, you tackle yet bigger things. And as you grow, you cannot but serve others, and you serving them results in them serving you, because this is how the development of consciousness works. In the spiritual world like attracts like, and giving attracts more giving, and you being in the flow means you participating in the abundance that is apparent wherever you turn, whatever you pay attention to.

ABOUT THE EXERCISE

This time it's about understanding that happiness and harmony are mental states of mind and not dependent on material wealth. That said, you are by no means rejecting material wealth; quite the opposite, in fact. You are using it to lift yourself onto even higher planes of life and existence, and this process is what you are really after. Think about it: as a spiritual being, as Charles Haanel wrote, you will not derive lasting satisfaction from material things, but they are means to an end and should be seen as such. And as your life doesn't end with what we call our physical death, but rather makes space for newer and richer experiences, your journey doesn't end there either, but is but a step in an evolutionary process of spirit that you are only beginning to fully comprehend and appreciate.

Please also include the material, plant and animal kingdom in your thoughts of harmony. Also include the higher worlds of devas, elves and angels. Our responsibility extends to them too, and our recognition of this will speed up our own process of enlightenment. It also assists in our appreciation of worlds other than our own.

CHECKLIST

1. Write down why you do not get disturbed when things seemingly go wrong.

2. Indicate on a scale from 1-10 how you've felt this week.

	Previous Week	Now
Your self-confidence:	_____	_____
Your energy level:	_____	_____
Your happiness:	_____	_____
Your drive and determination:	_____	_____
Your health:	_____	_____
Your wealth:	_____	_____

3. Write down why wealth should be a means rather than an end.

4. What are the three steps to creative power?

   1.
   2.
   3.

5. "Use governs existence." Please explain this statement.

6. Check which items apply to you

   ☐ I am whole.
   ☐ I am perfect.
   ☐ I am strong.
   ☐ I am powerful.
   ☐ I am loving.
   ☐ I am harmonious.
   ☐ I am happy.

7. If applicable, please write down what prevented you from checking all boxes above. (Remember Part Four where you have learnt that the real Self cannot be anything but perfect!)

8. What does the vitality of a thought depend on, and why is that so?

9. What role do mental images play in the creation of an ideal? Why do they have to be scientifically true?

10. Review point 28 and meditate with emphasis on the fact that persons, places or things have no place in the Absolute. Learn to understand that the Absolute is formless, but that persons, places and things are forms, hence material, whereas your goal is to pursue immaterial things like happiness and harmony.

11. Review point 33. It is of paramount importance, especially when it comes to the power of visualisation.

12. Write down some insights you have gained from doing the exercise.

NOTES

17

Intuitive Perception through Concentration

This week marks the beginning of the 5th month of studying. It's quite an accomplishment, so please accept my best wishes and congratulations! Not many have the discipline and tenacity to engage in a home study of this nature, but those who do will be richly rewarded - and have been already by virtue of their studying alone.

This week we are dealing with "intuitive perception through concentration". This mouthful of a statement is once again easy to understand when you have the right information, so here it goes.

Charles Haanel tells us that all great things come to you in silence and you are also at our best when we don't engage the Conscious Mind but rather intuitively rely on your subconscious faculties. He uses the example of an actor, who completely identifies with his role and delivers a superb performance. This actor is not thinking or analysing, but just doing it. He does it because he knows how to. Now when you seek the Silence, you aren't acting, but you are just as much calming the usually restless Conscious Mind and open the doors to your Subconscious. This way you really open and widen the channel, allowing for an increased information intake, past the Conscious Mind and straight into our Being. The Conscious Mind would never be able to process such amount of information in such a short time, but as your intention is positive and life-affirmative, you don't need to engage the 'Watchman at the Gate' to slowly sift through all the information that you are being saturated with.

On a scientific level, when you are in this state of meditation, something interesting happens. You raise your brain's alpha frequencies. One major 'tone' is at about 7.83hz; it's the so-called Schumann Frequency, which is at the same time is a standing wave that travels 7.83 times per second around the earth in the so-called earth-crust-ionospheric cavity. Technically you are becoming part of a closed resonance system that - if you remember what I said about them in previous parts - transfers a lot of information with very little input on your behalf. And this is exactly what is happening here. While concentrating and meditating and calming your senses, you raise your alpha frequency and allow for your being inspired and intuitively informed. The Universal is breathing through your very Being!

Every successful person hasn't just worked like a mad-man, but always taken time to seek solitude, to go into the Silence, and there allowed his or her thoughts to dwell on one particular thing only. This way the personal consciousness could grow. Charles Haanel makes several references to the importance of finding solitude and taking time off to "think" in an environment free of disturbances. Make it a habit too, and you will be surprised by the results.

You learn in this part that the vibrations of the spiritual forces are the most powerful. Compare the high frequency of your mobile phone to your vocal chords and you know what I mean. That said, the much higher vibrations of our thoughts can and will soon outdo the vibrations of the mobile phone and make that and many other technology relying on this redundant. Watch this space, as it is already happening, where telepathy is becoming commonplace.

You also learn that spiritual insight can only be gained when concentrating, and this insight tells you that an acceleration of consciousness is necessary. Remember what I said about that when I referred to the Maya Calendar? This acceleration takes place when we meditate and concentrate, and entertain an uninterrupted, focused and harmonious train of thought. As insight is of paramount importance, you will immediately understand the significance of last week's exercise.

Concentration on one particular thing or topic implies letting go of other thoughts. In fact, the moment we do concentrate, we automatically let go of such thoughts, because otherwise concentration would be impossible. Remember that this process helps us imprint new information onto the Subconscious Mind with the necessary "force", although concentration itself is totally effortless. As manifestation is largely subconscious, your learning how to concentrate teaches you how to manifest. Nice one!

ABOUT THE EXERCISE

Nothing needs to be added here, as it is about a complete letting-go and relaxation, followed by an intense concentration, which we do not confuse with physical or mental effort, but with becoming one with the subject of your concentration. Once one with it, you feel it, live it, strengthen it and assist the process of physical manifestation in the outer world.

"When you get to the heart of things, it is comparatively easy to understand and command them", Charles Haanel writes in point 31, only to substantiate this in the following paragraph.

CHECKLIST

1. Explain why physical power is becoming meaningless.

    _____

2. Indicate on a scale from 1-10 how you've felt this week.

	Previous Week	Now
Your self-confidence:	_____	_____
Your energy level:	_____	_____
Your happiness:	_____	_____
Your drive and determination:	_____	_____
Your health:	_____	_____
Your wealth:	_____	_____

3. How can an acceleration of consciousness be accomplished?

    _____

4. Why should concentration not be confused with effort?

5. Why does conscious desire seldom lead to the materialization of the object?

6. Check those items that apply or that you have performed this week:

    - [ ] I finish everything that I have started.
    - [ ] I enjoy doing the work I am doing.
    - [ ] I am grateful.
    - [ ] I know that my body is the Temple of the living God, and I treat it accordingly.
    - [ ] I spend time in silence, concentrating on my ideals, visualising them, feeling them.
    - [ ] I treat my desires as already accomplished facts.
    - [ ] I am becoming aware of my move from the headspace to the heartspace.
    - [ ] I regularly return to previous parts in order to absorb new wisdom contained in it.

7. In which way can we escape or emerge from limited success?

8. Why does the thought have to be converted into tangible values?

9. Write down why it is so important to think big thoughts and develop an appreciation of higher things?

10. How do you activate and then cultivate your intuition?

11. Why is it so important to seek silence and solitude?

12. What does "becoming inspired" mean to you?

TIPS

- ▶ Remember that the main practical goal of the Master Key System is to get you out of your head and into your heart. It's about developing and utilizing your intuitive faculties.
- ▶ On that note, the main intellectual goal is to know the Truth, so that you can apply it in your daily life.

NOTES

18

The Law of Attraction

Ah... "The Law of Attraction", topic of this 18th week, to which I would like to welcome you. In Part Five you've already learned that this Law doesn't bring you what you want, what you desire or what someone else has, but it brings you "our own". Your own is what comprises your predominant mental attitude, technically speaking: that which you have been continuously thinking about, and which has become so strong that it now resonates with like thoughts, thus reinforcing and increasing it, or "making more of it". Sound follows thought, and is the precursor of form, and according to the different vibrations, material patterns form and therefore the building blocks of matter.

Growth is the only thing that differentiates you from the Universal, because this is no longer growing. It simply is, resting, static, pure potential, substance in balance.

Your personality is nothing but your relation to the Whole, as you define yourself through this Whole. Remember: you are the channel through which the Universal expresses itself, and therefore grows in form. In itself it is not able to express itself in form. It always needs an outlet, and you are the conscious outlet, conforming to Natural Laws and thus living a life in abundance.

Intelligence is what shows your power to direct your actions and to consciously adapt to changing circumstances. Remember that circumstances will always change, as there are nearly infinite "beings" at various levels of existence at work to experience themselves - above you and below you. It is your understanding that allows you to tune into them and to make your mental vibrations rule or attune yourself to the physical manifestations of those other beings. Your mental appropriation, however, is always harmonious, systematic and constructive. Thinking is the invisible connection through which the Individual communicates with the Universal. Thinking is the dynamic phase of consciousness, which in itself is static - the aforementioned substance in equilibrium.

You learn in this part that only the belief that can be proven is of any value, and that can be considered "the living truth". All else is superstition and doesn't help you at all. Let go of it!

You also learn that growth is conditioned on reciprocal action, so if you don't ask the question, no one will answer. If you do ask, the Law of Attraction will "excite" the infinite potential of the Universal and bring it into manifestation through the Law of Correspondence, the Law of Vibration, the Law of Cause and Effect, the Law of Polarity, the Law of Gender, and therefore all the Hermetic Principles. And as inner wealth is the secret to outer wealth, you need to give in order to receive. But not give every now and then, but make that giving your predominant mental attitude. Give not because you have to or because someone tells you, but give because you can!

Also remember that Men has constantly been honing his tools, in order to accomplish more. We wouldn't know about the age of the Universe if it wasn't for the telescopes that were invented and built. The same applies to your own tools, your wonderful Conscious Mind, and the marvellous and infinite capabilities of the Subconscious Mind.

Finally, you learn in this part that power comes from a power consciousness, and its application or use. Without consciousness, there is no use. Without attention, there is no use. Without use ,there is no meaning for anyone or anything. The motivation or intention for your attention is your interest in this thing, your burning desire to find out more, to gain more insight, make new experiences, and therefore live life the way it is meant to be lived. And if you live it harmoniously, it will show ever so clearly in your physical, emotional and mental constitution. But more about that in the coming weeks.

ABOUT THE EXERCISE

The exercise of this week teaches you to grow with the demands that life places on you. You are concentrating on your power to create. You are asked to let your thought dwell on the fact that the physical Man lives and moves and has his being in the sustainer of all organic life, air, that he must breathe to live. The spiritual Man that you are lives, moves and has his being in an even subtler energy which he must depend on for life.

You see that this week's exercise places new demands on you. Charles Haanel also mentions the breath on which your organic life depends, so you are advised to read his book "The Amazing Secrets of the Yogi", which sheds more light on important breathing techniques and the Yoga Philosophy in general.

So please approach this exercise with the necessary diligence and seriousness, so that you can master it too and thus gain additional insight into the true nature of your Being.

CHECKLIST

1. Explain what it means to recognize the Self as an individualization of the Universal Intelligence.

   _____
   _____
   _____
   _____
   _____
   _____

2. Indicate on a scale from 1-10 how you've felt this week.

	Previous Week	Now
Your self-confidence:	_____	_____
Your energy level:	_____	_____
Your happiness:	_____	_____
Your drive and determination:	_____	_____
Your health:	_____	_____
Your wealth:	_____	_____

3. Explain why the creative Power does not originate in the individual.

   _____
   _____

4. What is the invisible connection, that the individual uses to communicate with the Universal?

....

5. "The only belief that is of value is one that can be put to the test." Why?

....

....

....

6. Check those items that apply or that you have performed this week.

   ☐ My connection with the Universal Intelligence is becoming deeper and more profound.
   ☐ I can concentrate better on whatever I focus on.
   ☐ I can visualize new things and add any detail to it that I can think of.
   ☐ I can physically sense situations and their energies.
   ☐ I recognize my role as Man in the evolution of Mankind.
   ☐ I am aware of my responsibility towards other beings.
   ☐ I am grateful for the many new insights I have received by studying the Master Key System.
   ☐ My physical fitness is in line with my mental developments.
   ☐ I find peace and contentment within myself.
   ☐ I have control over my emotions.

7. On a spiritual level, like attracts like. Why is that so?

....

....

8. Why is it so important to enter your heart space?

....

9. Recall the role of the Solar Plexus and its task as the 3rd chakra.

10. What does power depend on?

11. What does attention depend on?

TIPS

- In order to develop an appreciation of the big things, you need to first appreciate the small things. Make an effort to consciously look at things that you would normally ignore. You will become aware of unusual details. The more details you recognize, the larger your appreciation for all that is.
- When you drive to work in -say- a Northerly direction. Imagine you being somewhere else and driving West. Feel the difference in energy by this simple change in perception. This helps you look at the same thing with different eyes, something that you will be engaging in more and more.
- Ophiel, in his book I recommended some weeks ago, writes about the "sphere of Availability". He explains that for a beggar a rug or a jacket is within his sphere of availability, whereas a car is not, because practically he needs the former more than the latter.
So spend some thought on this and find out whether what you have set your sights on is really within your sphere of availability. If not, change your ideal, and have faith that it is up to you to expand this sphere of availability.

RECOMMENDED READING

- „The Hathor Material: Messages from an Ascended Civilization" from Tom Kenyon and Virginia Essene is a fascinating and enlightening read, complementing your MKS studies.

NOTES

19

Developing your Vital Force

We learn that fear is a powerful thought form that can be overcome by becoming conscious of our own power. It is exactly this sense of power that you will be developing in this part by concentrating on courage. So simple, so effective.

Remember, this is week 19. In the previous weeks you have spent hours concentrating on particular states of mind, so fear will be overcome easily by us focussing on courage. Where there is courage, fear must go.

Life Force or Vital Force is a central topic for each of us, because what is the point of honing your mental skills when your body falls into neglect, when you don't have the energy it takes to accomplish great things, the very things you have been visualising for weeks and months, and have imbued them with love so that they became alive.

Your physical power has to match your mental power. Mental power is only of value if it is being used. In order for you to use it, you need the physical strength and stamina to convert thoughts into powerful action.

Make sure that you exercise regularly and only take in unprocessed, nutritious foods. They both are means that your body needs to function well, just as much as fresh air, coupled with deep and rhythmic breathing.

This, too, is not accomplished overnight, but is a continuous process that will lead you from one level to the next, from one challenge to the next. The good news is that it gets easier. The real challenges are at the bottom end, and the more adept and equipped you become mentally, emotionally and physically, the easier you will master all tasks given to you.

The search for the truth is a logical and systematic process. To look for the truth means to look for the ultimate cause. This requires you to look beneath the surface (Part Eight), become aware of the rare and unusual things and to open your mind to the presently unknown. This way fate and luck make way for scientific principles, logic and reason. That said, these conscious and therefore mental processes are meant to become subconscious and therefore out of your mental reach - always remember this! The entire process of the development of Consciousness is not meant to bloat your brain and bog you down in analytical processes. It is meant to engage you in a process that is at first conscious, but through practice (read: repetition) becomes habitual, automatic, and then finally subconscious. This way the mind is freed from this task and can direct its attention at yet other things. Once again: this is a process of flowing and becoming, not a process of increased doubt, confusion and mental paralysis.

You will also learn in this part that Spirit is the only effective principle. Matter is only a condition that Spirit assumes and is therefore prone to constant change. Nothing material lasts forever – it is not meant to last forever!

You will learn that all extremes are relative, they are two parts of a whole. What Charles Haanel is talking about here is the hermetic principle of *Polarity*, so please also refer to the Kybalion to obtain further information. It will allow you to transform, transcend and transmute any unfavourable condition by focussing on the polar opposite.

Interesting in this context is also the fact that spirit grows through use, whereas Matter is consumed through use. That said, spiritual activities require material tools, in our case food and drink and air. Therefore another appeal to review your dietary habits and your state of physical fitness.

That which you think will show up in your state of health, for your body is nothing but a result of your thoughts and what you have inherited. But each cell has intelligence, so it is once again up to you to inform this cell correctly, read: truthfully. Your thoughts will also show in your business relations and your environment. Wealth is the result of Power. Spiritual power is superior to physical power, as it exists on a higher plane; it vibrates on a higher level. The realization of this will make physical power meaningless, and you will find the source for all power in your state of mind. Enjoy!

ABOUT THE EXERCISE

This week's exercise is about you becoming so absorbed in the object of our desire that you are conscious of nothing else. We are talking about total concentration here, a daunting task for the uninitiated, but an easy one for you, who has been diligent with all the exercises thus far. Also become aware of the fact that appearances are deceptive, for they are effects and therefore void of principle. Understand that they are the result of past thinking, and if unsatisfactory, they can be transformed by creating new causes. These causes are always spiritual at first, then mental, then emotional, and lastly physical.

CHECKLIST

1. Explain how fear can be overcome once and for all.

2. Indicate on a scale from 1-10 how you've felt this week.

	Previous Week	Now
Your self-confidence:	_____	_____
Your energy level:	_____	_____
Your happiness:	_____	_____
Your drive and determination:	_____	_____
Your health:	_____	_____
Your wealth:	_____	_____

3. What are you looking for when you are looking for the Truth?

4. What will your experiences with this newly gained knowledge from now on depend on?

5. Explain what it means that both extremes of any given thing are relative.

6. Check those items that apply or that you have performed this week.

    ☐ I understand that there is responsibility but not guilt.
    ☐ I am consciously directing my attention at those things that have principle.
    ☐ I am cooperating with other people in order to reach my goals.
    ☐ I am communicating in a clear and concise manner.
    ☐ My speech is harmonious.
    ☐ I refrain from gossip and speculation.
    ☐ I seek out places and people that are conducive to my ideals.

7. Why is Spirit the only effective principle in existence?

8. *"All wealth is the offspring of power; possessions are of value only as they confer power. Events are significant only as they affect power; all things represent certain forms and degrees of power."* Explain the meaning of this statement.

9. Explain the principle of polarity and how you apply your understanding of this principle in your daily life.

TIPS

> Our calendar determines our consciousness. However, our calendar is linear whereas our consciousness develops exponentially. This is why it is advisable to realign ourselves using the Tzol'kin Calendar of the Maya. This asynchronous rhythm of 13 and 20 helps us with this realignment and the new energies and insights that we are meant to absorb and integrate into our daily life. You will find more information on www.lucita.net and www.calleman.com.

RECOMMENDED READING

> I very much enjoyed *Osho's* books, his irreverence, insight, clear thought and sense of humour.

NOTES

20

Thinking as the True Business in Life

"Thinking as the true business in life" is the title of Part Twenty, which also marks the end of your fifth month of studying. Once again congratulations on this achievement. You are among a few yet growing number of people who show the stamina and determination to finish the studies and to reap rewards beyond their imagination.

You learn in this part that they only faculty that spirit possesses is the ability to think, and that all forms and shapes are a result of mental processes. Thinking therefore precedes action - first the spiritual, then the material.

Spirit only becomes active or dynamic, once you recognize it and its infinite possibilities. All great things come to you through recognition, and you are no exception. They will come to you, too, when you start recognizing them. First the intent, then the attention, then the awareness, then the ideal, followed by the visualization, the emotions, your actions, and finally the materialization.

If thinking is the true business of life, then power is the result. The real secret of power is an understanding of the principles, powers, methods and combinations of spirit, and a perfect understanding of your relationship with the Universal Consciousness.

All principles are changeless, otherwise they wouldn't be principles, and while the Universal can only act through the Individual, you quickly realize that the essence of the Universal is already present within you - you are this essence. This realization leads to real power and strength, as you are no longer looking for it on the outside, but find it inside of yourself.

Perception can only be developed in silence. To be inspired means to get off the beaten path. It is the art of imbibing, the art of self-realization; the art of adjusting the individual mind to that of the Universal Mind. For you this means more time in silence, more time spent dwelling on your thoughts, observing yourself, your thinking, speaking and your actions.

Wherever you look these days, the following pattern emerges:

First the knowledge - then the trust, belief or faith that what you desire has already been accomplished - then the application: the action to turn your belief into a living truth. Then you know that and how the process works, motivating you to aim even higher. And thus you will reach ever new planes of existence, because you possess the Master key!

You learn in this part to increase the demand. If you do, the supply will follow. This is a generally unappreciated fact. The Infinite is called such because it is infinite. It holds as potential everything you can possibly think of. And once you engage in this methodical process of thinking, you will turn dreams into realities.

Again, Charles Haanel makes us aware of Pranic Energy, Chi, Mana, Orgone, Aether or whatever you prefer calling it, that we take in when we breathe, which is why it is so important to engage in deep and rhythmic breathing. If you have neglected this part so far, please put this on your priority list and follow through!

ABOUT THE EXERCISE

Once again we go into silence and concentrate of the fact that "In him we live and move and have our being" is literally and scientifically exact!

At this advanced stage it won't take you long anymore to realize this, and also come to an understanding of the infinite possibilities at your disposal. It is you alone who is responsible for you physical, emotional and mental wellbeing. Being responsible, however, is no longer seen in a negative light, but as a challenge, as a chance to develop, to unfold, to experience, to live life on higher planes of existence.

CHECKLIST

1. Write down why the sceptre of power is consciousness.

2. Internalize why "good" and "bad" are based on one principle only.

3. Indicate on a scale from 1-10 how you've felt this week.

	Previous Week	Now
Your self-confidence:	_____	_____
Your energy level:	_____	_____
Your happiness:	_____	_____
Your drive and determination:	_____	_____
Your health:	_____	_____
Your wealth:	_____	_____

4. What does the recognition of the Spirit of a thing bring into manifestation?

5. What is the true occupation in life and what is its result?

6. What is the secret to all Power?

7. What happens if you consciously increase the demand?

8. Check those items that apply or that you have performed this week:

- [ ] My thinking is sovereign, noble and harmonious.
- [ ] I think first before I speak.
- [ ] I meditate regularly and am going into solitude.
- [ ] I find it easy to concentrate on "insight".
- [ ] „Negative" remarks from other people leave me unaffected.
- [ ] I have made someone an unexpected present.
- [ ] Every day I feel my conscious connection with the Omnipotent.
- [ ] I am the love, health and wealth that I deserve.
- [ ] I am good enough to live an abundant life.
- [ ] I am courageous and action-driven.

9. Look up point 20 and meditate on Haanel's statement about consciously breathing with intent.

10. What is this Cosmic Energy and how can it be activated?

11. What does the quality of the circumstances that we have created for ourselves depend on?

12. How can our permanent wellbeing be assured?

TIP

> These past weeks we have learned to concentrate. Prior to that we have learned to use our imagination. Most of these tasks have put your Conscious Mind to the test and expanded your awareness. Now try the exact opposite and just "be". Don't think,

reason, argue, analyse - just be. This is a real expression of power and control over yourself and therefore your Being. Here you take a conscious decision not to interfere but allow something to develop, while you are merely observing. This provides you with important insights, which you would not have gained if you had judged and tried to manipulate the issue based on your judgment.

NOTES

21

Thinking Big Thoughts as the Secret of Success

"Thinking big thoughts as the Secret of Success" is the title of this part. It deepens your understanding of the interaction between consciousness and the application of its power.

You will learn in this part that the real secret of power is a consciousness for power. Consciousness is being developed by paying attention, by becoming receptive to the finer details in life.

If you look back at the last five months, do you notice a change in the scale of your thinking? Are you thinking bigger now? Have you set yourself bigger goals, created bigger ideals, or are just more confident that you will accomplish bigger things than before? Now remember that this "bigger" is not in comparison to others, but in comparison to yourself. You are the one growing. You are the one with the desire for more health, wealth and happiness. So go back five months - with all the exercises under your belt, this will be an easy task - and recall who and how you were back then, how you thought, and what you thought was possible or not. Notice a change? If not, you are well advised to return to the beginning of your studies. If you do, you are to be congratulated.

Knowing that the Universe is governed by law, that there is an effect for every cause and cause for every effect, helps you to think, and to think big on top of that. By thinking big you are creating a demand, and as you have learned in the previous week, a higher demand creates a higher supply. So big thoughts create big supply. And as you think anyway, why not think big right away? Trust me, the Universe won't mind. :)

As you become aware of your inherent power, you become more energetic, more driven, yet also more serene and sovereign. Your application of the knowledge you have gained makes you more powerful, and through this application more things come to you. Once again, power is nothing without application. Continental, the tyre manufacturer, once used the slogan: "Power is nothing without control", and this is equally true, as the real secret of power is a power consciousness and therefore your conscious control of it.

You learn in this part that big ideas have the tendency to eliminate small things. Your enriched mental world increases your mental, emotional and physical capacity, and this way you become capable of accomplishing big and valuable things. Please ponder on this for a while and compare it to what you have learned in Part Eight about looking beneath the surface.

If you keep doing the same things, you will keep receiving the same things. So if you want a change in your outside world, you will only realize this with a corresponding change in your inner world. No esoteric doctrine here, just pure science. If you are not yet fine-tuned to appreciate the finer things in life, only the rough stuff will register with you. But it's in the finer details, the lesser known things, that the true value resides. That's why you are on this journey of becoming more sensitive and receptive to them. Your black-and-white view is changing to one of many-splendid colours. A new vision appears before you, glorious and radiant, beckoning you to make it real. So go right ahead! Demand increases supply, remember?!

ABOUT THE EXERCISE

This week you will learn to concentrate on the truth. As you spend time doing this, you once again absorb more information and wisdom, gain additional insight, and through its application gain further power and strength, thus lifting yourself and Mankind onto a new level. Dwell a little on this and also recall the Hermetic Principle of Polarity. Remember that although there are two poles, they are just variations of one thing, of one principle. Remember that if your mind is limitless and without obstacles, so will your outside world. It is this truth that shall set you free, but that's the topic of the 24th and final part, which we will tackle in a couple of weeks time. For now, be diligent with this exercise and concentrate to the best of your abilities on the truth by making use of your intelligence and insight and understanding of the Natural Laws.

CHECKLIST

1. Write down what needs to be present in order to imprint something onto your consciousness.

2. Indicate on a scale from 1-10 how you've felt this week.

	Previous Week	Now
Your self-confidence:	_____	_____
Your energy level:	_____	_____
Your happiness:	_____	_____
Your drive and determination:	_____	_____
Your health:	_____	_____
Your wealth:	_____	_____

3. What governs the Universe?

4. What is the result of our thinking?

5. What happens when we become conscious of our oneness with the Universal?

6. Big ideas push aside small ones. Why is this statement scientifically true?

7. Check those items that apply or that you have performed this week:

    ☐ Another person changed their behaviour towards me.
    ☐ I am thinking BIG thoughts.
    ☐ I am aware of how my past thinking has led me to where I am today - in all aspects.
    ☐ I am aware of the support that is available to me wherever I turn.
    ☐ I can physically sense this newly developing power in me.
    ☐ I consciously decide what I am paying attention to.
    ☐ The exercises are part of my daily studying regime.
    ☐ I feel the love of my fellow beings.
    ☐ I am aware and can feel the love I am showing towards myself.
    ☐ My life is great.

8. Name the Law that brings us our experiences?

9. How do we change external manifestations?

10. The creative thought is being determined by your ideal. What determines the passive thought?

11. The divine Spirit makes no exceptions. Explain why this is so.

12. What is the Almighty in and by itself?

RECOMMENDED READING

 📖 Gregg Braden's "*The Divine Matrix*" is another excellent read, so are his other books. Very enlightening and encouraging.

TIPS

- ➤ Thinking "big" is made easy when you look at the results of your past thinking and then ask yourself if you couldn't have done better and what prevented you from reaching this. This is not about performance issues or oneupmanship, but about you reaching the goals you have set for yourself in an orderly and structured manner. It is about an honest assessment of yourself and the foundation of the development of your consciousness.
- ➤ Remember that all great thoughts come in silence. If necessary, refer to Part 17 how to obtain intuitive perception though concentration.
- ➤ Mingle with people that - to you - represent or live that which you desire to live. Buy magazines that connect you with that same energy. Visit the websites, connect to the respective Facebook pages..., there is just so much you can do to tune into new energies and qualities.
- ➤ Write down below what you are going to do now in light of the above information.

NOTES

22

New Thinking, New Man

"New Thinking, new Man" is the title of this part. Hardly surprising after now 5 months, is it? In silence and meditation you have grown from a primitive thinker at the whim of anything from planetary constellations to other people's opinions, to your own uncontrolled emotions, to a cool, calm, collected, sovereign, compassionate and empathetic Human Being. Step by step you have unfolded your potential. You are in the process of becoming an outstanding personality. People seek out your advice, feel drawn to you, and assist you in getting more of what you yourself desire to have more of. Remember that your personality is defined by our relation to the Whole.

Gone are the times of fate, luck, chance or caprice, of emotionality, ups and downs, incalculability, dependency, irrespective of people, organisations or other external circumstances. It is you who is setting new causes in motion, and these causes are in alignment with your ability to express them, coupled with your understanding of yourself and the Natural Laws that govern the Universe.

You don't pay attention to the outside world, knowing it is the world of effects, not causes.

Your physical, mental and emotional power reflects your efforts made over the past months and takes form in beautiful, orderly, harmonious and well-meaning things. You are fulfilling your role as a conscious co-creator and Creation rewards you abundantly. You are deserving it because of your hard mental work and trust in the process.

It is through your thinking that you continuously redefine yourself. This part deals with your health. It reminds you that negative emotions cause disease, dis-ease – the absence of ease. Negative thoughts have the tendency to damage and destroy the nervous and the glandular system. It is obvious then that you cannot but think positive and harmonious thoughts. You need to create an image of physical perfection, and keep that image in your mind until you have imprinted it on your Subconscious Mind. It is always the same procedure: from belief to knowledge, from consciousness to subconsciousness, from the Brain to the Solar Plexus, and eventually to your heart.

Without good health, no amount of money will be of use to you. So the knowledge you gain in this part lays the foundation for the next one, where you will be learning about the money consciousness in service of Mankind.

The Law of Vibration is what leads you to perfect health. Vibration precedes materialization, and when you aren't happy with the latter (the effect), it is obvious that the former (the cause) needs adjusting. This is being effected through the power of visualization. New images create new imprints, and new imprints create new realities.

As you can see, it is always about your choice to think the right thoughts, say the right words and do the right things. You have been prepared, or rather… you have prepared yourself well over the past months. As a result, you are now able to express far more than just a few weeks ago.

Very importantly, you will learn in this part about how your Conscious Mind impacts on your body, but that not of a lasting nature. You will also learn how the Subconscious Mind's actions on the body differs. As soon as something unusual happens, the intelligence inherent in every cell of the body is called upon and kicks into action in order to correct the "mistake". All this happens without your knowledge or conscious intervention. You quickly realize the devastating effects on your entire Being when the Subconscious Mind has been supplanted and sabotaged by false thinking. You will realize just as quickly how important it is to only think beauty, love, and harmony, because this is what you are going to manifest. This is what all your desires are about at the end of the day.

ABOUT THE EXERCISE

This week you will be concentrating on a quote by Lord Alfred Tenneyson, *"Speak to Him, thou, for He hears, and spirit with spirit can meet. Closer is He than breathing, and nearer than hands and feet."* Understand that when you speak to "Him" you are in touch with the Omnipotent. *"The realization and recognition of this Omnipresent power will quickly destroy any and every form of sickness or suffering"*, as Charles Haanel says. When you focus on this quote, please recall what you have learned about the Conscious Mind's impact on the body in comparison to the Subconscious Mind's actions. If you internalise this well, you will find it easy to stop relying on your Conscious Mind, while using it for its intended purpose. The "Watchman at the Gate" has to be on full alert until you are subconsciously taking all the right decisions.

CHECKLIST

1. Write down the two modes of operation that keep you alive.

2. Indicate on a scale from 1-10 how you've felt this week.

	Previous Week	Now
Your self-confidence:	_____	_____
Your energy level:	_____	_____
Your happiness:	_____	_____
Your drive and determination:	_____	_____
Your health:	_____	_____
Your wealth:	_____	_____

3. What is the source of all disease and sickness?

4. What does your current physical condition depend on?

5. What needs to be done to reach physical perfection?

6. What do we change when we change the rate of vibration?

7. Spirit exercises control over the body using which Law?

8. Which Law is used to obtain perfect health?

9. What is being activated when we have progressive, courageous, noble, constructive and friendly thoughts? How are they expressed in form?

10. Why is it indispensable for us to provide the Subconscious Mind only with perfect images?

11. How does a higher rate of vibration effect a lower one?

12. Check those items that apply or that you have performed this week.

    - [ ] My life has changed completely in the past 22 weeks
    - [ ] I am disciplined.
    - [ ] I can visualize great goals and know how to reach them.
    - [ ] My fellow human beings are supporting my endeavours.
    - [ ] Synchronicities take place more often than in the past.
    - [ ] I have obtained my ideal weight or are about to obtain it.
    - [ ] I am much stronger and much more flexible than at the beginning of my studies.

- ☐ I have become conscious of old patterns and now know how to dissolve them and let them return to their Source - the Light.
- ☐ I hold no grudges against other people. I forgive them and send them much love.
- ☐ I surround myself with people who are on the same wavelength.

RECOMMENDED READING

- 📖 Charles Haanel's „*A Book about YOU*" connects ancient wisdom with modern thinking and scientific methods. It explains the various forms of vibration and how they affect our life. It explains how the planets affect us and which chakras they are connected with.
- 📖 If you want to know more about correct, rhythmic breathing, his book "*The amazing Secrets of the Yogi*" is an excellent choice. There are also modern books that give you an introducing to the Yoga Philosophy, but if you like Haanel's style of writing, this one is it.

EXERCISE

Write down one or more things that you are going to tackle and bring to fruition in light of the newly gained knowledge and skills. Call them 'new ideals'.

1.
2.
3.

NOTES

23

Serving Mankind with a Money Consciousness

A very interesting topic awaits us: money! Charles Haanel intentionally left it this late, while I am sure most would have loved this topic to be dealt with right at the beginning of the Master Key System. The reason for only dealing with it now no longer requires an explanation, but for those who are unsure, allow me to add the following:

For more than five months now this course has prepared you. It has taken you into the depths of your own Being, brought you into touch and conscious co-operation with the Omnipotent, and therefore imbued you with powers and qualities previously undreamed of. You are now a completely changed person, with more insight, more intelligence, more compassion, wisdom, and capabilities to express life in a completely new way. Now, with this as a foundation, we tackle the subject of "money".

As you perhaps know, the chapter titles were added by myself - the original didn't have any. When I did this right in the beginning of the German translation, I confess that I didn't really know what I was doing. I just looked up a phrase or keyword that would summarize the essence of the respective part, and this part, too, was titled in this manner. Rightly so, I am sure you will agree with me, and rightly so that Charles Haanel deals with this subject only at the end of this course. If he had done so prior, you would have lacked vital information and experience. Now, however, it's a different story, and you are enabled and capable of making the most of this trade medium we call "money". So go right ahead and...

In this part you will learn that money is a means, not an end. You will learn that you are not after the money itself, but the state of consciousness that it affords you. As a spiritual being ,you will not find lasting satisfaction in material things, but they help you attain the desired level of happiness and harmony. With money you can make happen so much more than without money. You can partake in international trade, in providing goods or services to people, thus serve and enrich them.

You see, the whole notion of money for the sake of money was never a healthy and sustainable one, because just making money would make you empty on the inside. But far from negating money, we are using it as a tool and a means to be of service to others. Remember what Charles Haanel said about the telescope. Not so long ago we could just spot the moon and a few planets. But as we developed stronger telescopes, even placed them in the sky, we were able to look much deeper into the sky and therefore into our own origins. The same you will be doing on a different scale. Whatever your product or service, it will benefit and enrich people. It will help them become healthier, wealthier or more loving. You can no longer take advantage of their own ignorance. You know that this energy will first go through you and leave a trail of physical and emotional destruction, before it can reach someone else – and that person may still be able to refuse this energy and project it back at you, with dire consequences.

For close on six months now you have been taken by the hand and guided into a new life. Now use money to make more money for others, and let it return to you manifold, or use it until you don't need it anymore. That's also perfectly fine.

Nature produces in abundance wherever we turn our eye. By developing a money consciousness we enter the flow that is constantly flowing anyway. We aren't creating anything new; we are tapping into something already existent. We make a conscious decision to partake rather than to abstain. And if you don't like the effects of the current use of money, well, that's what your beautiful brain and the power of your imagination are there for. Dream up, think up, talk up, act up new visions of a better and healthier flow of money, goods and services for the benefit of Mankind. Leave behind a legacy of generosity and harmony. You already have the key, now put it in the door and open it!

Give generously, because it forms and shapes your consciousness. Giving is a spiritual activity. Only money can change hands materially. All other giving is a giving of the mind and the heart. As soon as I realized this, a huge weight fell off my shoulders. No longer did I have to have it in my physical presence in order to give it. All that was needed was my mental appropriation, my making use of it, and by using it I developed a consciousness for it, and thus became more and more powerful. And the more I used it, the more it came back to me. With each cent spent on a new service or product, more came back to me - in form of more cents, but also more friends, love and appreciation. And all the while my consciousness kept growing, kept increasing, and still is. You can and you now will do the same; not because I say so, but because you **can** and you **want** to!

ABOUT THE EXERCISE

This week you will concentrate on money as a means, on spiritual rather than material things. When you realize that you need to create a multiple of what you want to receive in the end, feel free to recall the subject of the past weeks, where you were dealing with the "development of your vital force" as well as with "thinking big thoughts as the secret of success". For example, if you want to make 100.000 dollars, you need to create a value chain to the tune of –say– 800.000 dollars. After all deductions of tax, production costs, shipping and handling, middlemen, etc., you will get your share. If you are using the Internet, it may be 400-500,000, but still far more than you will keep for yourself.

Not clear? Well, where should the 100.000 come from if not from others who have decided to pay for your goods and services? These have to be created and moved from you to the customer, or you have to engage in some other service that creates new value. This sets in motion a chain that enriches those who are part of it. You in turn are left with a good margin for yourself. However, this means that you must set your sights much higher than just the 100,000 you want for yourself. You have to think much bigger, and the resulting action will then bring you the 100k for sure. In the process, though, you have enriched others and now they are enriching you. Life is great, because with your right thinking, right words and right actions are making it great. You are the creator of it, and you can be proud of it! And never forget to be more interested in the journey than the destination. It's a ride, a fun ride to boot, so don't get too serious about that stuff, ever.

CHECKLIST

1. Write down the "major thought" of the Universe and its implications on your own life.

   _____

   _____

2. Indicate on a scale from 1-10 how you've felt this week.

	Previous Week	Now
Your self-confidence:	_____	_____
Your energy level:	_____	_____
Your happiness:	_____	_____
Your drive and determination:	_____	_____
Your health:	_____	_____
Your wealth:	_____	_____

3. What is the opposite of a poverty consciousness?

   _____

4. What is the first Law of Success and what does it build on?

   _____

   _____

5. What is your challenge in relation to the fickle and inconsistent forces of life?

6. What is your first step to becoming a money magnet?

7. "*What benefits one, must benefit all.*" Why is that so?

8. Why is it so important to think independently and for yourself and not allow others to do the thinking for you?

9. What is the most practical thing in existence, that a person can only hope to find?

10. Why does the Universal have no objection against your mental appropriation of spiritual laws?

11. Explain the meaning of money in relation to your desired circumstances.

_____

_____

_____

TIPS

> If money is an issue for you, ask yourself what prevents you from having more money. Look at wealth with open and honest eyes. Observe how you react when it comes to rich people or obvious signs of material wealth. Is it affirmative or negative? That shows with what you are in alignment with.
> Always focus on harmony and happiness. These emotional states are what you are after, not the material possessions. The former is spiritual and therefore permanent, whereas possessions are manifestations and therefore of no permanence. They are means, but not an end.
> The same is true for love. Love just is, irrespective of people and circumstances. Do not confuse your ego's flawed comprehension and its worldly desires with the true state of bliss that is Happiness and Harmony, Acceptance, Tolerance and Compassion.

RECOMMENDED READING

- Catherine Ponder's *"The Dynamic Laws of Prosperity"* is an excellent and motivating read and explains more about how to attract material wealth into our life.
- Florence Scovel Shinn's *"The Game of Life And How To Play It"* is similar to Catherine Ponder's book. You can also get all of Florence's wisdom in one single book on Amazon.
- There are countless books on how to get rich, but ask yourself if this is what really gives you happiness, or if it isn't rather something else. In any case, money will always remain a means, not an end.

NOTES

24

The Truth shall set you free

Before I say a few words on this last and final part of the Master Key System, I would like to pay you a huge compliment for staying put, for reading and internalising its contents, for filling out the checklists, and for applying your newly gained knowledge in your daily life.

I would like to congratulate you on creating a more glorious, radiant and beautiful version of yourself, for pushing limits, exceeding limitation, rejecting lack and limitation, fate and luck, and for assuming responsibility for your own life.

You are now in possession of everything you require to live a new life – a life in health, wealth and happiness. Charles Haanel provided you with all the necessary information. The only thing I know of that he left for you to figure out yourself was the issue of thankfulness, or gratitude. But I told you, so there. Sure, you will read other books, participate in seminars or go to talks, learn more about the history of Mankind , the workings of the Solar System, Yoga, and so much more, but these are all extras. You now know who you really are and how you are connected with everything in existence.

Perception creates reality. Perception creates connectedness, because how would you be able to perceive something if you aren't connected to that which you are perceiving? You and I are One, but not only you and I. We are all one. We are all expressions of this one Universal Intelligence that pervades all things, material or otherwise. The realization of this fact will lead to compassion and understanding, to love and helpfulness. It will lead to beauty and harmony, because "**I am(,) that(,) I am**",[1] and now, after six months of studying the Master Key System in detail, how could you entertain any thoughts other than those of love, beauty, and harmony? You know you can and sometimes still do, but you know you don't want to, and you will make the necessary efforts to remove even the slightest hint of negativity from your Mind and soon your entire Being. Practice makes perfect, but this practice first starts in your head, and ends in your heart.

You know you have a massive advantage over those who are not privy to the information conveyed in the Master Key System. But far from taking advantage of this, you will be helping them wherever you can. Whether "they" want to be helped or not is again something you decide, referring you to points 9-13 in this part. Read and understand them well.

You will learn in this part that it is the truth that shall set you free. I am sure you've heard this saying before, but now you know what is behind it. Perhaps for the first time it makes sense to you.

You have come to realize that you are living in an absolutely fantastic time. It's a time where so much comes true so quickly. Billions of souls have incarnated to assist in the Evolution of Consciousness. Yes, they are here for a reason! This process is now in its final stages and is accelerating fast. Too fast for some, but just right for those who have acquired a consciousness for it. They are able to recognize the patterns, get certainty, become centred, obtain peace of mind and make intelligent decisions.

We live in a time where for the Maya, one World comes to an end, and another one begins. We live in a time where we are concluding one Large Platonic Year of almost 26.000 years. In June 2012 there is also a rare Venus transit. It will most likely be the last one you will watch, for there are only two per century – the first one taking place in 2004.

You are very privileged to live in such times. You are very privileged to have access to such information and be able to act on it. You are privileged to have been given the Master Key System, in order to make this wisdom yours and to use it for the benefit of all involved.

Let love flow into everything you do. Tackle it with courage and determination, with faith and belief, and turn this belief into a living truth,

---

[1] Place the commas wherever you prefer, and the expression takes on a slightly different meaning. Meditate on all three combinations.

one that you know for sure, because it can be repeated again and again. It is then when we will have left the realm of superstition, of outside control, luck and fate, and have taken our life into our own hands. As a result, a reality has opened up to us that exceeds all our expectations. Sure, we will still have to learn lessons, but now with the Master Key at hand, we know exactly how we have to proceed. We will even know what to do when turmoil arises. Turmoil always arises at critical junctures, but they are necessary to establish a new system or order.

Idealization, visualization, love, feelings, action; thinking as the dynamic phase of spirit, connecting the Infinite with the finite; the use of practice (repetition) to imprint new patterns onto the Subconscious Mind, thus freeing the Conscious Mind from 'boring routine' and allowing it to dwell on new things yet again.

What an amazing system, this Human Body, and what a marvellous thing this 'Mind' is, that we have been given! Absolutely wonderful!

ABOUT THE EXERCISE

This week it's really only about obtaining clarity that this is a wonderful world we live in; that you are a wonderful being; and that many awake to these wonderful truths about us and this grand system of Creation; and as soon as they awake and obtain the knowledge, they will become aware of all the splendour that is awaiting their ears and eyes, and they will find themselves in the Promised Land.

Once again, please take the necessary time for this exercise to become aware of the amazing beauty, the abundance, love and all the wonderful opportunities for you to learn and become enlightened.

As a "Master" of your mind, you have become the Master of your Solar Plexus and are now ready to dwell in your Heart space. It's the fourth chakra and has different tasks and different responsibilities. But first you had to master the third one, which was why you came to the Master Key System in the first place.

CHECKLIST

1. Write down why you have to first give to life that which you wish to receive, before you will receive that which you desire.

2. Indicate on a scale from 1-10 how you've felt this week.

	Previous Week	Now
Your self-confidence:	_____	_____
Your energy level:	_____	_____
Your happiness:	_____	_____
Your drive and determination:	_____	_____
Your health:	_____	_____
Your wealth:	_____	_____

3. Why can we not rely on our senses?

4. Why is every form of suffering, disease, lack and limitation a form of erroneous thinking?

5. What sets those apart who are in possession of health, love and wealth from those, who aren't?

6. Name the correct method for the elimination of any kind or error.

7. Name the correct method for helping others.

8. Why are circumstances void of a true reality?

9. What is indicating the progress that we are making?

10. What is the product of logical training?

11. What does it mean to think truthfully?

12. Check those items that apply or that you have performed this week.

    - [ ] Other people are fulfilling my requests or wishes. These requests of mine are always harmonious.
    - [ ] I am of service to Mankind.
    - [ ] There are no undesirable situations anymore. They simply are.
    - [ ] I have to concern myself less and less about what I have think, as it is now part of my Subconscious Mind.
    - [ ] The opinions of others are important to me, but I always make my own.
    - [ ] I am consciously directing my Subconscious where it is still needed.
    - [ ] I am making other people happy, which in turn makes me happy!
    - [ ] My breathing is harmonious, deep and rhythmic.
    - [ ] I regularly seek the Silence and Solitude in order to find insight and intuition.
    - [ ] I am fully aware of my oneness with the Universal.
    - [ ] My nutritional diet is harmonious and life-affirming. I absorb the light and I radiate the light.
    - [ ] My physical constitution is to my liking. I am full of energy; my body is supple and flexible.
    - [ ] I give thanks to all that is.
    - [ ] I am overflowing with love. All those who meet me are being filled with that same love.
    - [ ] My material wealth is to my liking. I share it with my fellow beings, feeling happy and content.
    - [ ] I am fully aware of my divine nature and am looking forward to all the tasks that lay ahead.

FURTHER READING

- 📖 Gopi Krishna writes beautifully about "*The Awakening of Kundalini*". As you have been practicing rhythmic breathing for a while now, you will become interested in the subject of chakras, Kundalini and the raising of your life force.
- 📖 If you find old theosophical readings, many of them are real treasure chests with much insight into the workings of the World and the workings of Man.
- 📖 If you are interested in a book of incredibly high energy, read P.G. Bowen's "*The Sayings of the Ancient One*", Rider 1936. His words will certainly touch and move you. You can purchase it on www.masterkeysytem.tv.

UNLOCKING THE DOOR...

- ☐ I have obtained the Master Key when I have absorbed the wisdom of these teachings and am applying them in my daily life.
- ☐ I have understood that I can only express powers that I possess.
- ☐ I have understood that I am a spiritual being in a physical body having a life experience, which I can consciously determine with every breath I take. Argument, Visualization and Auto-suggestions are methods of finding the truth.
- ☐ I have understood that thoughts create things as spirit is creative, and that the heart of any given thing is its spirit.
- ☐ I have understood that infinite resources are at my disposal, and that they are waiting for my appropriation.
- ☐ I have understood that I am the temple of the living God, and that in order to accomplish great things, I need to keep this temple clean: mentally, physically and morally.
- ☐ I have understood that the intelligence doesn't originate in me; I am merely a conscious channel of divine energy expressing itself through me.
- ☐ I have understood that Idealization is the first step, followed by visualization, followed by your feelings and treating your wish as an already accomplished fact. Let there be no distance between you and your desire!
- ☐ I have understood that the valuable things are those least frequently noticed; that it requires careful observation beneath the surface.

- [ ] I have understood that everything in this Universe is subject to Law, and that my compliance with the Law brings to me the enjoyment of the best that life has to offer.
- [ ] I have understood that as much as I can get more of a given thing by paying increasing attention, I can also withdraw its vital-force by refusing to pay attention to such thing.
- [ ] I have understood that this Infinite Power is impersonal and enables me to use the correct method of thinking for my own benefit and that of all involved.
- [ ] I have understood that power is meaningless without use.
- [ ] I have understood that any great things comes through an increased reliance on my intuitive faculties.
- [ ] I have understood that the first law of success is service; that I am here to serve, and the more I serve others, the more others serve me.
- [ ] I have understood that everything exists in my own consciousness; that healing has to take place there, rather than on the outside; that I have no patient but myself.
- [ ] I have understood that this journey is just the beginning of a much greater one, but that this one has to be mastered first.

Congratulations! May the Master Key open all the doors you deem fit for unlocking. Use it wisely, and be blessed with a life abundant! It's been a pleasure serving you. – Helmar Rudolph

Made in the USA
Middletown, DE
15 June 2019